Teach Yourself
VISUALLY™

Scrapboo

D0118008

Scrapbooking

Visual

by Rebecca Ludens and Jennifer Schmidt

WILEY

Wiley Publishing, Inc.

The publisher and the author make no representations or warranties with respect to the accuracy or completeness of the contents of this work and specifically disclaim all warranties, including without limitation warranties of fitness for a particular purpose. No warranty may be created or extended by sales or promotional materials. The advice and strategies contained herein may not be suitable for every situation. This work is sold with the understanding that the publisher is not engaged in rendering legal, accounting, or other professional services. If professional assistance is required, the services of a competent professional person should be sought. Neither the publisher nor the author shall be liable for damages arising here from. The fact that an organization or Website is referred to in this work as a citation and/or a potential source of further information does not mean that the author or the publisher endorses the information the organization or Website may provide or recommendations it may make. Further, readers should be aware that Internet Websites listed in this work may have changed or disappeared between when this work was written and when it is read.

For general information on our other products and services or to obtain technical support please contact our Customer Care Department within the U.S. at (800) 762-2974, outside the U.S. at (317) 572-3993 or fax (317) 572-4002.

Wiley also publishes its books in a variety of electronic formats. Some content that appears in print may not be available in electronic books. For more information about Wiley products, please visit our web site at www.wiley.com.

Library of Congress Control Number: 2005939195

ISBN-13: 978-0-7645-9945-3
ISBN-10: 0-7645-9945-3

Printed in the United States of America

10 9 8 7 6 5 4 3 2 1

Book production by Wiley Publishing, Inc. Composition Services

Praise for the Teach Yourself VISUALLY Series

I just had to let you and your company know how great I think your books are. I just purchased my third Visual book (my first two are dog-eared now!) and, once again, your product has surpassed my expectations. The expertise, thought, and effort that go into each book are obvious, and I sincerely appreciate your efforts. Keep up the wonderful work!

—Tracey Moore (Memphis, TN)

I have several books from the Visual series and have always found them to be valuable resources.

—Stephen P. Miller (Ballston Spa, NY)

Thank you for the wonderful books you produce. It wasn't until I was an adult that I discovered how I learn—visually. Although a few publishers out there claim to present the material visually, nothing compares to Visual books. I love the simple layout. Everything is easy to follow. And I understand the material! You really know the way I think and learn. Thanks so much!

—Stacey Han (Avondale, AZ)

Like a lot of other people, I understand things best when I see them visually. Your books really make learning easy and life more fun.

—John T. Frey (Cadillac, MI)

I am an avid fan of your Visual books. If I need to learn anything, I just buy one of your books and learn the topic in no time. Wonders! I have even trained my friends to give me Visual books as gifts.

—Illona Bergstrom (Aventura, FL)

I write to extend my thanks and appreciation for your books. They are clear, easy to follow, and straight to the point. Keep up the good work! I bought several of your books and they are just right! No regrets! I will always buy your books because they are the best.

—Seward Kollie (Dakar, Senegal)

Credits

Acquisitions Editor
Pam Mourouzis

Project Editor
Donna Wright

Copy Editor
Lynn Northrup

Editorial Manager
Christina Stambaugh

Publisher
Cindy Kitchel

Vice President and Executive Publisher
Kathy Nebenhaus

Interior Design
Kathie Rickard
Elizabeth Brooks

Cover Design
José Almaguer

Cover and Interior Photography
Matt Bowen

Special Thanks...

We would like to acknowledge all of the scrapbookers whose work was chosen to be displayed in the book. Your creativity is astounding and your scrapbook pages are gorgeous.

- Tracey Eller
- Jennifer Foster
- Veronica Johnson
- Neith Juch
- Michon Kessler
- Vicki Lockmiller
- Candy McSween
- Jennifer Okonek
- Shiela Scott
- Mindy Tobias
- Jenna Tomalka

Special thanks to our models Carolyn Meyers and her daughters Alana and Julia.

About the Authors

Rebecca Ludens (Kalamazoo, MI) is the Scrapbooking Guide for About.com, where she writes weekly articles, product reviews, and how-tos. She has created scrapbook page designs for several scrapbooking manufacturers and has appeared on the television show *DIY Scrapbooking* and at scrapbook shows, retreats, and cruises.

Jennifer Schmidt (Crystal Lake, IL) has been on the design team for several scrapbooking manufacturers. She has been teaching scrapbooking classes for over eight years at conventions across the country, and has had pages published in scrapbooking magazines as well as having pages displayed on *DIY Scrapbooking.*

Acknowledgments

Thank you to all the photographers, both professional and amateur, who allowed us to use their photos on scrapbook pages in this book: Shea Wetzler of Shea Photography, Linda Curtin, Carolyn Meyers, Dara Ludens, Julie Gehring, Heidi Lachel, and Barb Obley.

Thank you, also, to our husbands (Douglas Ludens and Brian Schmidt) who were so patient and supportive during the process of writing this book. And, of course, thank you to our children (all eight of them between the two of us) who are our constant scrapbooking inspiration—Bethany, Lindsey, and Mikhail Ludens; Elizabeth, Kaitlyn, Rachel, Steven, and Philip Schmidt.

Table of Contents

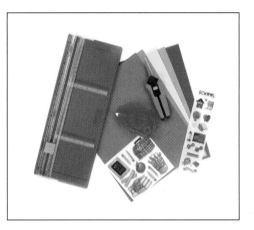

chapter 3 Create a Scrapbook Page

chapter 4 Select Colors for Your Scrapbook Pages

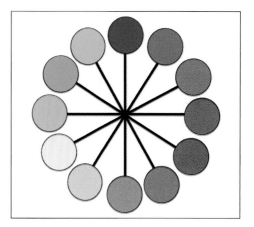

Matting Essentials

Journaling Styles

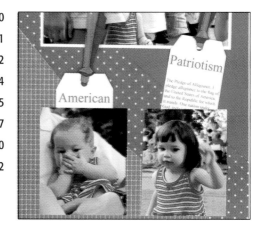

chapter 7   Designing from Page Plans

chapter 8   Title Tricks

 **chapter 9** Paper Techniques

 **chapter 10** Three-Dimensional Embellishments

chapter 11 Working with Wire

chapter 12 Get Organized

chapter 13 Mini and Theme Scrapbooks

chapter 14 Photo Inspiration

chapter 15 Layout Gallery

chapter **1**

Getting Started

Preserving family, vacation, and heritage memories in scrapbooks is an extremely rewarding hobby. To get started on your first scrapbook, take some time to understand the types of supplies available to you and how to choose the best materials for your project.

Why Scrapbook?

Understanding why scrapbooking is important to you and deciding what your purpose is in scrapbooking determine the types of supplies, embellishments, and album that you use.

Reasons for Scrapbooking

PRESERVE YOUR PHOTOS

Many pictures that have been put into photo albums over the last 50 years have been damaged by the harsh chemicals used in the adhesives in those albums. Scrapbookers need to use materials (paper, adhesives, and inks) that will not damage photos in order to preserve them for future generations.

SAVE YOUR MEMORIES

Photos without journaling are memories for only a short time. Soon the names, places, and event information are lost and only a photo remains. The heritage photos (family pictures from previous generations) shown here have no memories associated with them because the names and information about these people have been lost over time.

RECORD MAJOR EVENTS

Weddings, graduations, birthdays, holidays, and anniversaries are among the many life events that easily lend themselves to scrapbooking.

RESEARCH OF YOUR FAMILY HISTORY

Genealogy study and even just looking up the basics of your family tree can be the perfect time to start scrapbooking. Documenting this information in a scrapbook will allow future generations to benefit from the knowledge you have gleaned of your family's heritage.

REMEMBER THOSE PRECIOUS EVERYDAY MOMENTS

Not every photo you take will be of a major event in your life. Most of them will be the little things. These everyday pictures will be treasured in your scrapbooks for years to come.

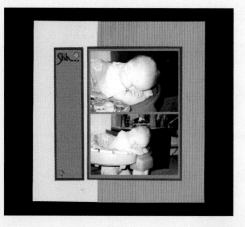

Scrapbooking with Children

Children are naturally creative. Including them in your scrapbooking provides not only quality family time together but also adds their unique perspective to your pages.

GATHER SUPPLIES

Keep it simple. Basic supplies such as a pair of scissors, an adhesive runner, a trimmer, paper, and stickers are all a child needs to get started. Store these basic supplies where they are readily accessible so that you can take advantage of any free time to work on some scrapbook pages with your child.

USE A SMALL-SIZE ALBUM

Smaller album pages require fewer photos and decorations to complete. These albums come in a wide variety of styles and colors, making choosing the album almost as fun as completing it.

MAKE COPIES

Giving your children copies of the photos they are working with allows them to have some creative freedom while giving you peace of mind.

ENCOURAGE JOURNALING

You will look back on these pages and enjoy seeing how your child grew and how their handwriting changed over the years. Help them decide what to write by asking them questions that relate to the scrapbook page. Their answers become the journaling text.

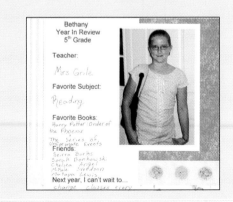

Theme albums are perfect for children. A theme album has a defined beginning and an end. It can be completed in a shorter amount of time than a regular chronological album. Following are some theme albums that work great for children; more theme album ideas can be found in Chapter 13.

ABC ALBUMS

ABC albums are theme scrapbooks where each page starts with a different letter. Larger books can cover the whole alphabet, while smaller books could cover just the letters in your child's name; for example, "What is special about RACHEL?"

ALL ABOUT ME SCRAPBOOKS

All about me scrapbooks are interview-style albums where children fill in information about themselves on each page; for example, "My best friends are . . ." "My favorite books are . . ."

TRAVEL/SPECIAL TRIP

Travel/special trip scrapbooks allow your child to record which events and memories were most meaningful to them. These albums may include photos, memorabilia, and journaling, all from your child's perspective.

SCHOOL PAGES OR YEAR-IN-REVIEW ALBUMS

School pages or year-in-review albums cover the events of a specific year. One album can cover the whole year, or you can simply add a couple of pages each year to an ongoing album.

Scrapbooks come in a variety of styles and colors. Each style is defined by a distinctive binding method. Looking at the pros and cons of each style can help you choose which one is right for your project.

POST-BOUND ALBUMS

Post-bound albums are bound by screws and posts. The page protectors are bound into the album and the pages slip into the protectors from the top.

STRAP-HINGE ALBUMS

Strap-hinge albums are bound by a plastic strap that passes through staples that are bound into the edges of the scrapbook pages.

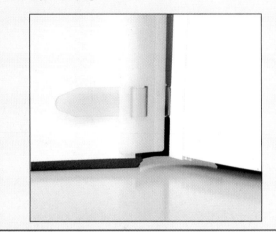

3-RING BINDING ALBUMS

Three-ring binding albums have a lot in common with a classic 3-ring office binder. For scrapbooking, you can find binders with leather and fabric covers. Top-opening page proctectors simply slip on the rings.

SPIRAL AND BOOK-BOUND ALBUMS

Spiral and book-bound albums can be simple and inexpensive, or elegant and pricey. These scrapbooks are usually chosen for a special project or gift album.

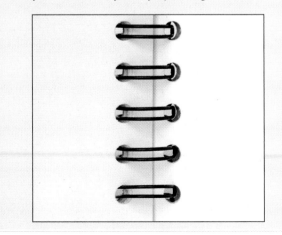

POST-BOUND ALBUMS

Advantages: The pages lie flat. The album is easily expandable by adding post extensions. Top-opening page protectors allow any type or color of paper to be used for each layout.

Disadvantages: You need to slip pages out of the protectors or remove posts to rearrange pages.

STRAP-HINGE ALBUMS

Advantages: Pages lie flat when open. Albums are expandable.

Disadvantages: Pages are bound by a strap, making it difficult to rearrange layouts. When the pages are bound to the book, you have to cover each page if you want a selection of backgrounds with each layout.

3-RING BINDING ALBUMS

Advantages: Rearranging pages is quick and easy. Several sizes of rings are available; choose a D-ring style for ease of use.

Disadvantages: The rings lie between the pages of a two-page spread when open. The albums are not expandable.

SPIRAL AND BOOK-BOUND ALBUMS

Advantages: Spiral-bound albums are inexpensive and great for working with kids. It's also easy to decorate the cover and the binding. Book-bound albums make professional-looking heritage and family albums.

Disadvantages: These albums are not expandable. You are limited to flat embellishments. Pages can't be rearranged or removed after they are completed.

Album Sizes

The scrapbook project you are working on determines the size album you need. The variety of sizes available will spark your creativity and get you thinking about all the different albums you could make for friends and family. The most common sizes of scrapbook albums are 12" × 12" and 8½" × 11".

Common Sizes

12" × 12" albums are most often selected for chronological or event-oriented family albums. The larger page size allows room for more photos and embellishments. Paper is available in a huge array of colors and styles in this 12" square size.

8½" × 11" albums also make great family albums; however, this smaller size makes them a good choice for a more defined album, such as a school album or a child's scrapbook. The smaller page size allows you to create great pages with fewer photos.

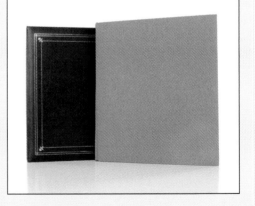

11" × 8½" albums are basically the 8½" × 11" album turned on its side. The long rectangular shape of these album pages makes them ideally suited for the classic 4" × 6" size of photos. This album is a fun alternative to the more traditional album sizes.

4" × 4", 6" × 6", and 8" × 8" albums are all varying sizes of the square page made popular by the 12" × 12" album. These smaller sizes are perfect for gift or theme scrapbooks. Fewer photos are required to complete each page, while the square shape works with the same design schemes as the 12" × 12".

Smaller and specialty albums are fun, complete-in-a-weekend-type scrapbooks that come in as many shapes and varieties as your imagination can dream up. Scrapbooks can be made from CD holders, tags, or even paper lunch bags (see Chapter 13). Some manufacturers are selling these tiny albums to add to pages or stand alone as mini-books.

Scrapbookers know it is all about the paper. The array of paper available for this craft is amazing. Choosing paper appropriate for your specific scrapbook project will be easier after this overview of paper types.

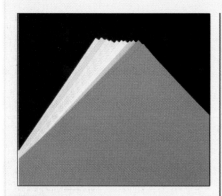

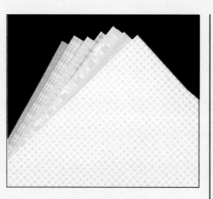

CARDSTOCK

Cardstock is a scrapbooking necessity. You could create entire albums with only different colors of this heavyweight paper. An easy way to coordinate cardstock is to purchase it in monochromatic sets of different shades.

PATTERNED PAPER

Patterned paper adds interest to your cardstock layers. This lighter-weight paper comes in every print imaginable. Pattern paper fills in the spots on your scrapbook pages that may look a little too plain.

SPECIALTY PAPER

Specialty paper includes vellum, mulberry paper, metallics, and meshes. You can print on vellum while still having the photo or colored paper beneath it showing through. When you tear mulberry paper, it leaves a fuzzy edge that can add an interesting texture to a scrapbook page. Just a small amount of metallic or mesh can add a significant level of texture and drama to a page.

Trimming, cropping, and edging are all fancy words for cutting up things in scrapbooking. Good scissors and a paper trimmer are a must. Shape cutters and punches make their respective tasks quicker and easier.

SCISSORS

Scissors are a scrapbooker's best friend. A good-quality pair of scissors with a nice sharp edge makes every scrapbooking task you do easier. Decorative scissors come in many different styles. One mistake that beginners sometimes make is cutting photos with decorative scissors. The fancy edge takes the focus off of the photo and puts it on the decorated edge.

PAPER TRIMMERS

Paper trimmers are a must for cutting sheets of paper and also for getting a good straight edge when you crop or trim your photos. A 12" trimmer allows you to cut any size paper. This is a tool that you will use every time you work on your scrapbooks.

SHAPE CUTTERS AND PUNCHES

Shape cutters and punches are used to cut paper and photos into a variety of shapes and designs. The most basic shape cutter can be used to cut circles and ovals of varying sizes. Punches come in every shape and size imaginable. Select some basic punches like geometrics (circles and squares) and tags that you will use again and again.

Choose Adhesives

Adhering photos and memorabilia to the pages is the main task in scrapbooking. When you shop in the scrapbook aisle at your local hobby store, you will find that there are many different types and styles of acid-free, scrapbooking adhesive. Choosing the right one makes all the difference in how your project turns out.

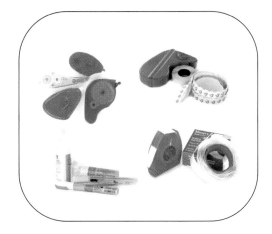

Styles of Adhesive

Tape runners will be your scrapbook friend. These versatile adhesive dispensers are the right choice for adhering both paper and photos to your album pages. Some tape runners dispense clear white strips, or even little blue dots of adhesive. Be sure to read the label. If you want to be able to remove items from your pages in the future, choose a "repositionable" adhesive; otherwise "permanent" is best.

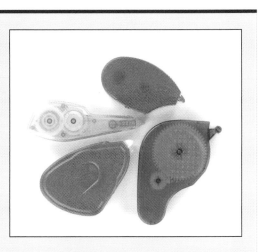

Photo tabs are small squares of white double-sided adhesive. Despite the name, they work on both paper and photos. Just one tab in the corner on the back of each photo is all you need. This adhesive also allows you to pop the pictures back off the layout if you need to remove them to make copies at a later date. To save time, purchase a photo tab dispenser, similar to how tape runners are sold.

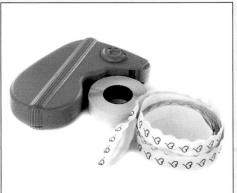

Adhesive dots come in a variety of sizes and thicknesses to suit the project. These little super-sticky dots are exactly what you need to adhere dimensional items to your layouts such as buttons, metal embellishments, and even fabric and ribbon strips.

Liquid glues and glue pens are good for specific uses such as metal embellishments and tiny items like letter die-cuts. Use liquid glues sparingly to avoid any spillover on other parts of your layout. Because liquid glues are permanent adhesives, you may not want to use them on your photos.

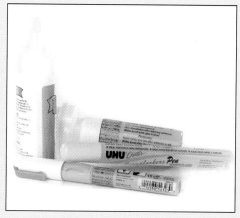

Adhesive machines are the fastest way to adhere die-cuts to your pages. Simply insert the item into the machine, turn the crank or pull the strip, and out the other side come items that are now turned into stickers. If you decide to use die-cut letters, an adhesive machine is a must.

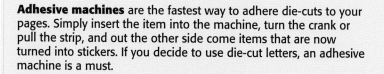

Tools for Journaling

Journaling is the process of writing down the thoughts and memories that go with your photos. Having the right tools for the job makes the writing process easier and ensures that your memories last as long as your scrapbooks do.

A BASIC BLACK PEN

Use a basic black pen to write on your pages either in a journaling box (a space created specifically to hold the text) or directly on the background cardstock. The pen you choose must be permanent ink, acid-free, and fade-resistant. You can choose from a selection of different tips to create bold, fine, or fancy lines.

PEN OR PENCIL FOR LABELING PHOTOS

Labeling photos may be part of your photo organization technique. The pencil or pen you use for this purpose should be designed specifically for the task. Do not use ballpoint pens; the ink will continue to bleed through the photo for years, eventually causing damage to the front of the picture. Soft photo labeling pencils are perfect for writing on the back of pictures.

MATERIALS FOR GETTING CREATIVE

Getting creative is the heart of scrapbooking. You can add creativity to your journaling with colored pencils, chalks, letter templates, rubber stamps, or a collection of pens in a range of colors and tips. The same rules that apply to the basic pen apply to these supplies: permanent ink, acid-free, and fade-resistant.

TIP

Basic Supply Checklist:
- ☐ Scrapbook album
- ☐ Scissors
- ☐ Paper trimmer
- ☐ Cardstock in a variety of colors
- ☐ Patterned paper
- ☐ Adhesive
- ☐ Basic punches: circles, squares, tags, corner rounder
- ☐ Black journaling pen

chapter 2

Your Photos

Great photographs are the essential element to fabulous scrapbook pages. Unfortunately, most of us would say that we don't take a lot of "great" photos. Without an organizational system, the photos that do happen to turn out wonderfully may be lost in boxes or piles. In this chapter, you learn how to take better photos and organize them efficiently.

Take Better Photos

Beautiful photographs are the most important part of an eye-catching scrapbook page. Taking better photographs makes scrapbooking easier and more rewarding.

Make Your Photos Better

REMEMBER THE RULE OF THIRDS

A simple rule of graphic design, the rule of thirds, can make both your photos and your scrapbook pages better. If you create an imaginary grid over the top of your photo or in your viewfinder that divides the picture in thirds horizontally and vertically, the places where the lines intersect are the focal points of the photo. Rather than making your subject the center of the photograph, try shifting just slightly so that the subject's face or eyes hit one of those intersections and you will have a better photo.

COME IN CLOSE

Fill your viewfinder with your subject. Many pictures are better if the person taking them simply zooms in on the subject. On scrapbook pages, the emotion of the photos can be seen when the subject is close up.

TAKE PHOTOS FROM VARYING ANGLES

Photos taken from above, below, and behind the subject can add interest to your pages and capture little details that you may have missed. Also, photographs of children are often stronger when taken from the child's eye level.

PAY ATTENTION TO LIGHTING

Movie directors know all about special-effect lighting. The light shining softly through a sun-lit window can create beautiful photos. Harsh overhead sunlight can create shadows on your subject's face. This can be corrected by using a flash even if you think you don't need one.

SHOOT IN BLACK AND WHITE

Sometimes colors in your photos can be distracting. The emotion of the photo can shine through when color is stripped away and we see the photograph in simple black and white. Black-and-white photos are fun to scrapbook with because you can use just about any color scheme to accent them.

Enlarge Your Photos

The layout shown here demonstrates how you can create a beautiful 12" × 12" scrapbook page with just a single photo. The key is to enlarge that photo to fill the space. By enlarging the photograph, the details become more important—the texture of the tree, the strand of hair blowing into her face. These details help tell the story of the scrapbook layout; thus fewer photos and less journaling.

The best and most beautiful things in this world cannot be seen or even heard, but must be felt with the heart.

Lindsey, your beauty is apparent to everyone who sees you, but your true beauty is deeper and shines from your heart.
Age 7 – May 2005

One of the easiest digital edits, and one most applicable to scrapbooking, is adding text directly to your photos. You can print the journaling, add a quote, or even insert the title directly onto a photograph. The scrapbook page on the opposite page shows how much impact a quote can have when it is added to an enlarged photo.

Open a photo in photo-editing software. Click on Type Tool or Insert Text (usually indicated by a single capital letter).

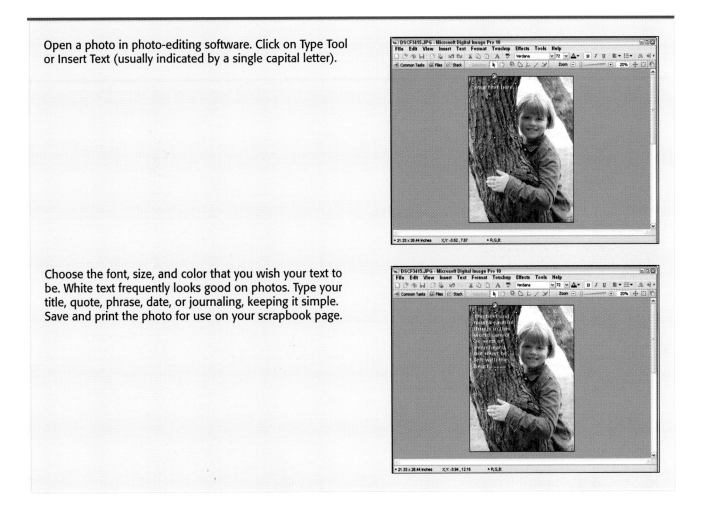

Choose the font, size, and color that you wish your text to be. White text frequently looks good on photos. Type your title, quote, phrase, date, or journaling, keeping it simple. Save and print the photo for use on your scrapbook page.

Repair Damaged Photos

Time, poor storage, and wear and tear can all have a detrimental effect on your precious family heirloom photographs. You can repair these ravages of time by scanning the photo into your photo-editing software and following some simple steps.

① Scan the photo into your computer at a high resolution—300 dpi or better. Save the image to a file on your computer and then open it in your photo-editing software.

② Zoom into the damaged areas of the photo—200% for single-color areas or 700% for multicolor areas of the photo—allowing you to see each individual pixel.

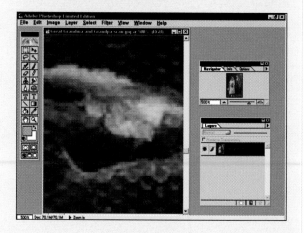

③ Use a selection tool such as Lasso or Freehand to select undamaged areas of the photo that match the colors that should be in the damaged areas. Usually you can select areas immediately adjacent to the damaged areas to copy. Click Copy to copy the selected area.

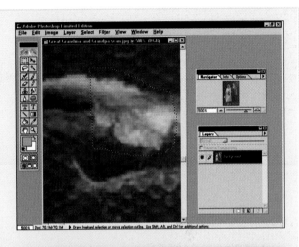

④ Click on the damaged area and then click Paste to cover up the damage. You may have to use your mouse to move the copied area to get it to line up just right over the damaged area. Repeat these steps until you have covered up all the damaged areas in the photo. Save and print the repaired image to add it to your scrapbook page.

CONTINUED ON NEXT PAGE

The gorgeous heritage photo on this scrapbook page was once the damaged photograph shown on the previous page. Now it has been returned to its former beauty. This page uses simple embellishments and soft colors so that the restored photo remains the focal point.

Two Become One

June 25, 1924

Alice Yearman & Hubert Schultz

Trimming or cropping photographs is one of the first things that most scrapbookers are taught. An important reason to crop a photo is to create a focal point for a picture by removing distracting images. The "before" layout below uses a photo that could be better.

Before: There is distracting clutter in the background of the photo.

After: Once the photograph is cropped and the focal point enlarged, it makes a much stronger statement. The background "noise" of the picture has been reduced so that you can focus on the little girl's face.

Crop to Include More Photos

Another important reason to crop photos is to fit more photos on a scrapbook page. Sometimes a story can be told with one photo; other times you need several. This scrapbook page shows that by cropping some of the photos to a smaller size and by printing others wallet size, you can get many photos on one layout.

Do not crop out all historically relevant sections of your photos. Also, do not crop one-of-a-kind or heritage photos. And never crop Polaroid photos. The chemicals in older Polaroid photos that cause them to develop will leak from the photo and can damage your albums. The scrapbook page shown here is extra-special because the car was left in the picture. These old family photographs make a great scrapbook page because they were not cropped.

Pride

Independence

Freedom

I doubt the feelings related to getting your first car have changed much over the years. Remember the feelings of independence and freedom. Steve looks so proud of his "new" car, a 1946 Chevy Club Coupe, bought for him by his Grandpa. If only it was still around today.

Steve Schultz--1946 Chevy Club Coupe-- April 1966

Organize Your Photos

Perfect photos are useless if you can't find them. The best organization method for your photos is one that you can maintain on a regular basis.

Methods for Organizing Your Photos

PHOTO BOXES

Photo boxes come in a variety of colors and materials, from bright floral cardboard to clear plastic. Basically this is a file-folder type of organization in which dividers are labeled and photos are grouped by date, theme, or subject.

Advantage: You can organize years and years worth of photos quickly.

Disadvantage: It is difficult for family members to enjoy the photos while they are in storage.

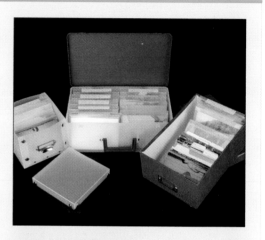

PHOTO ALBUMS

Photo albums don't have to become obsolete when you start putting your photos in scrapbooks. Rather, let photo albums become your organizational technique. Look for albums that are acid- and PVC-free and can hold a lot of photos. Some albums have room next to the photos for journaling. This is helpful for recording the basic facts of the events in the photos so it's there by the time you get around to scrapbooking.

Advantage: Family and friends can still view and enjoy the photos.

Disadvantage: It is time consuming to rearrange photos in this method.

DIGITAL STORAGE

Digital storage is the easiest way to store and sort photos for scrap-booking. Several software programs allow you to tag photos with keywords so you can sort them by subject, theme, holiday, date, or anything else you may come up with. Be sure to make regular backups of your photos on CD or other media to prevent loss in case of computer problems.

Advantage: You can store thousands of photos in very little space.

Disadvantage: You will need to print them out before you can start scrapbooking them, and it may be harder for friends and family to enjoy them while the photos are on your computer.

TIP

Disaster Recovery Preparation

Fire and natural disasters are two major ene-mies to your scrapbooks. Digital photo storage and some simple steps can help you be pre-pared in case your precious albums are destroyed.

1. Take digital photos of each of your scrap-book pages. The photos should be taken in bright natural light, at a straight-on angle so that the page is lined up squarely in the camera's viewfinder.

2. Save the digital photos of your scrapbook pages on CDs. Be sure to label each one indicating the title of the original scrap-book album from which the pictures were taken.

3. Store the CDs somewhere other than your home. Some "off-site" storage sug-gestions include: a safe-deposit box, a relative's house in another state or area, or a friend's house in another part of the country (you could trade with another scrapbooker—you store his or her CDs and he or she stores yours).

In a worst case scenario, copies can be printed from your digital images of scrapbook pages at your local copy center. Some places can even print on large format paper so that you could print a 12" × 12" copy of your lost page.

chapter 3

Create a Scrapbook Page

The hardest scrapbook page you will ever make is that very first one. Once you understand the parts that make up a layout and how to put them all together, jumping into creating your own pages will be much easier.

Scrapbook pages can be created in many styles with several different types of embellishments; however, they all break down into the same basic parts. Understanding these parts of a layout will guide you in creating your first page.

1. FOCAL POINT PHOTO

Select one photo that tells the main story of the page.

2. SUPPORTING PHOTOS

These photos support the main photo and complete the story without taking the focus off of the focal point.

3. BACKGROUND CARDSTOCK

A solid sheet of color is used here to be the foundation of the layout.

4. EMBELLISHMENTS (BUTTONS AND CUT-OUTS)

Simple decorations add to the theme of the page without distracting from the photos.

5. TITLE

A title defines the theme of the page.

6. JOURNALING BOX

Journaling is the words that complete the story—the emotions behind the photos or simply the who, what, when, why, where.

1. Gather the supplies that coordinate with your photos and your theme.

2. Decorate the background cardstock. Simple stripes were added to break up the color and add visual interest.

3. Decide where to place the photos on the layout.
4. Add title and journaling.
5. Add any desired embellishments. Pre-printed graphics, stickers, or dimensional decorations all make finishing your page quick and easy.

Great scrapbook pages catch the reader's eye. When planning a layout, remember that having a focal point, or a main photo, adds impact to your page.

In this layout, each photo has equal importance, or weight, on the page. The eye has nowhere specific to land, which creates a visual jumble.

Select a photo that can be enlarged or cropped to give it maximum impact on the layout and give your reader's eye something to focus on. This photo is your focal point.

Here the layout has a clear focal point photo. Notice how this gives the page a completed and professional feel.

Supporting photos have been narrowed down to just the best ones needed to tell the story of the page. Not every photo that you take needs to be put in your scrapbook. Pick the ones that best show the memories you wish to record.

Mikhail loves sports. In Spring 2005, he started soccer and can't get enough of it. His natural abilities are shining through, we can't wait to see how his interests grow and change as we watch him grow-up.

PRACTICE makes Perfect

Without words, the photos you take and save in your scrapbook will become meaningless in one generation. Journaling is the simple act of writing down the thoughts and memories that accompany your photos.

Journaling Styles

Handwritten journaling can have the most emotional impact on a layout. Your handwriting is part of who you are, and including this on at least some of your scrapbook pages is important.

In the layout shown here, family members each wrote in their own handwriting how they felt when they first saw the picture of the little boy they were adopting from Russia.

Computer-printed journaling will probably make up the bulk of the writing you do on your scrapbook pages. It's quick, easy, and creates clean and neat-looking pages. The two main advantages of using your computer are: spell checking and being able to re-size text to fit in a specific area of your layout.

This layout shows a "just the facts" style of computer-printed journaling. The text consists of simple main points that relate who, what, when, where, and why. Here the text simply tells the date and location.

CONTINUED ON NEXT PAGE

Letter-style journaling is a very personal style of writing. You express your thoughts and feelings about the photos as a letter to the person who is the subject of the pictures. An example of a letter used for journaling is shown in this father-and-son layout in which a moving tribute from wife to husband is recorded.

Great FUN good

Brian,

What a good daddy you have become. You have shown our children many things ... the silliness of a good joke ... the joy of tickles ... how fun it is to laugh ... the love in discipline ... the challenge of checkers and chess ... how to get lost for hours in a fun computer game (maybe this was inherited) ... the depth of your love ... and the faithfulness of your word.

I have often had people comment on how hard it must be on our kids that you travel for work. But although you travel our little ones know how much you love them, and how they can always count on you.

You have taken the time to get to know them. You have taken the time to get down on their level and play, even when they were small. They know that when you are home you have time for them. These things show in the joy they radiate in your presence.

The girls love to see you off on a trip by standing in the door and waving as you drive away. But even more they love to greet you when you return. You must delight in the cry of "Daddy!" upon entering the house and their little arms as they encircle you to give you hugs. It gives me great joy to see your love for them, and to see that love reflected back toward you.

I love you,
Jennifer

dada DAD Daddy papa

Creating a list is a journaling style that will work with a variety of pages. Made famous by late-night talk shows, "top ten" lists are perfect for jump-starting your journaling.

In the layout shown here, the designer lists the things that can be learned while playing miniature golf.

Life Lessons in

Keep your head down and your eye on the ball.

Putt firm not hard.

You have to know where the hole is.

Putt straight.

Follow through.

Golf with friends it's more fun.

Stay on the course so you don't get a penalty.

Stay out of the sand traps because it is really hard to get back out.

Watch the person in front of you, if they do well do the same if not try a new approach.

Miniature

GOLF

CONTINUED ON NEXT PAGE

Poems and quotes can be especially helpful when you are at a loss for words to accompany a certain set of photos. Here the beautiful pictures of a botanical garden are accented by an excerpt of a poem entitled "Spring."

Cheekwood Botanical Garden
Nashville, Tennessee, June 2004

grow   bloom   create

I know not which I love the most, Nor which the comeliest shows, The timid, bashful violet Or the royal-hearted rose: The pansy in purple dress, The pink with cheek of red, Or the faint, fair heliotrope, who hangs, Like a bashful maid her head.

by Phoebe Cary in *Spring*

joy

Question-and-answer-style journaling uses the title of the page to begin the text by asking the question. The rest of the journaling on the page answers the question and explains how the photos relate to the theme of the layout. On this summer fun layout, pictures of summer activities are tied together with this style of journaling.

What do you like to do in the summer?

Reading a good book.

Piano lessons.

Summer Fun

Zoo trips.

Riding bikes.

Swinging at the park.

Playing at the beach.

Embellish Your Layout

Photos and journaling are the essential elements of any scrapbook page; however, creativity starts to emerge as you select the items that you use to embellish, or decorate, your layouts.

STICKERS

The most basic scrapbook page embellishment is the sticker. Stickers come in an enormous variety of styles, colors, and shapes.

Three-dimensional stickers take the basic sticker to the next level and add a finished look to your layouts.

DIE-CUTS

Cardstock cut into shapes and letters by a machine using shaped dies are called die-cuts. You can use pens, chalk, ink, or other materials to decorate these simple embellishments and give them extra flair.

You can purchase die-cuts, or you may eventually wish to invest in a personal die-cut machine and dies to cut out your own shapes and letters.

PRE-MADE EMBELLISHMENTS

Manufacturers in the scrapbook industry know that you have a limited amount of time to spend working on your pages. They sell more and more pre-made embellishments, which include everything from intricately detailed titles to tiny albums that allow you to add more photos and journaling to your layouts.

DIMENSIONAL ITEMS

Adding dimension to your layout is like adding an exclamation point to a sentence—it finishes the page with punch! Items such as buttons, fibers, and plastic gems add that finishing touch.

ATTACHMENTS

Brads, nailheads, and eyelets are the basics in a variety of embellishments known as attachments. These decorations can stand alone to decorate a page or can be used to attach other items or layers to the layout.

chapter 4

Select Colors for Your Scrapbook Pages

Color is the beginning of creativity with scrapbook pages. Choosing colors that work well together *and* complement your photos can be a challenge. Learning how to select colors makes your scrapbooking not only easier but also more fun.

Use a Color Wheel

In your first art class in elementary school, you probably learned about the color wheel. This simple device demonstrates the relationship of colors to each other and can be especially useful to scrapbookers.

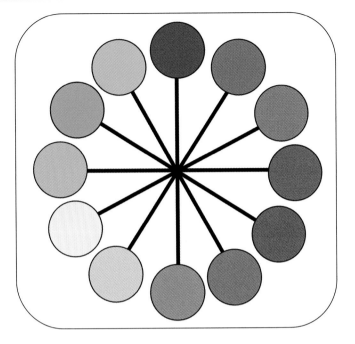

MONOCHROMATIC COLOR SCHEMES

Monochromatic colors are varying shades of the same color. Layouts that use a monochromatic color scheme can complement most photos and are easy to select. A simple trick for selecting monochromatic colors is to use paint strips found at your local home improvement or hardware store to select the shades you wish to use on your layout.

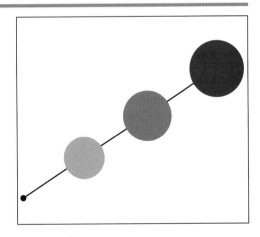

This layout uses varying shades of purple that accent the baby's bow. An advantage of monochromatic color schemes is that the colors tend to fade to the background, allowing the photos to be the main attraction on the layout.

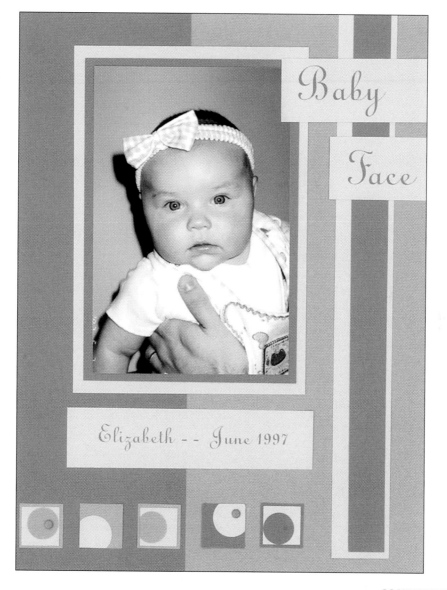

CONTINUED ON NEXT PAGE

ANALOGOUS COLOR SCHEMES

Analogous colors are two colors that are right next to each other on the color wheel. This color combination is as easy to select as monochromatic, and having two colors adds extra interest to your layout.

The page shown here uses blue and blue-green as an analogous color scheme.

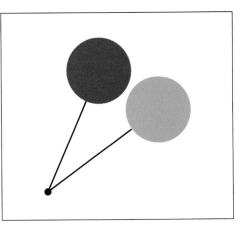

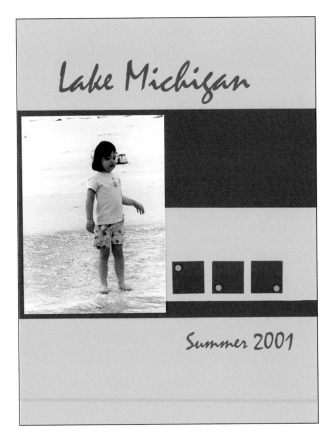

TRIADIC COLOR SCHEMES

The primary colors of red, blue, and yellow are equidistant from each other around the color wheel, dividing it into thirds. These colors make up what is known as a triadic color scheme. Any three colors that are exactly one-third of the color wheel away from each other will work together nicely on a scrapbook page.

In the layout shown here, the colors purple, green, and orange are used as a triadic color scheme. To give balance to the layout, one color (orange) is chosen as the dominant shade and the other two are used as accents.

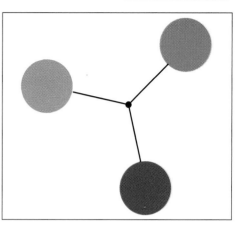

Birthday Wishes

Bethany turns twelve.
August 2004

CONTINUED ON NEXT PAGE

COMPLEMENTARY COLOR SCHEMES

Complementary colors are those that reside directly across from each other on the color wheel. These colors are in sharp contrast to each other and can add some extra "pop" to your layout.

The layout shown here uses a complementary color combination of blue and orange. Matching the shade of the colors when you combine them is an important part of all color schemes. Light blue and light orange are used on this layout.

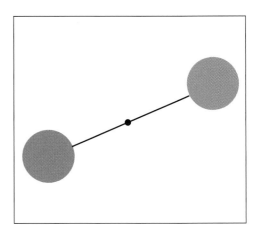

SPLIT COMPLEMENTARY COLOR SCHEMES

Split complementary color schemes are a variation on the classic complementary color scheme. This time you select your first color and then use two other colors that are an equal distance away from the complementary color of the first. This combination has more balance without as much contrast as the complementary color scheme.

Yellow-orange and red-orange are contrasted by blue in this split complementary color scheme scrapbook page. Adding the third color gives significant visual interest to the layout.

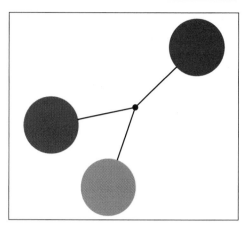

Maddie — June 29, 2000

Let's Read

CONTINUED ON NEXT PAGE

TETRADIC COLOR SCHEMES

When you combine two complementary color pairs, you have a tetradic color scheme. This can be a difficult combination with which to achieve a pleasing balance. To avoid the competition between the colors, simply select one color to be the main color, and use the others as accents.

The layout shown here uses green and red with blue and orange as two complementary contrasting pairs, creating a tetradic color scheme. To maintain balance on the layout, blue is the dominant color and the other three shades are used as fun accents.

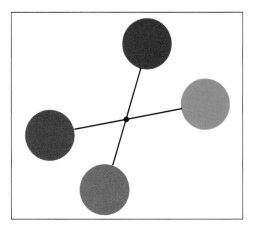

Pool Fun

May 26, 1998

There is nothing quite like a dip in the
pool to cool off on a hot summer day

Color can help tell the story of your layout. Bright, warm colors can reflect a playful party. Cool, calm colors create a quiet, reflective mood. The layout shown here uses neon shades of primary colors to make an exciting beach page.

At the Beach
Lindsey has always loved swimming, so it makes complete sense that one of her very favorite places is the beach.

CONTINUED ON NEXT PAGE

This layout shows the exact same photos with a cool monochromatic color scheme. Notice how the feel and mood of the layout is affected by the color choices.

At the Beach

Lindsey has always loved swimming, so it makes complete sense that one of her very favorite places is the beach.

Color schemes are useful tools for selecting colors. Once you have selected the colors, how do you decide how much to use of each one? This quick color rule helps you achieve balance on your scrapbook pages.

Gallon, Quart, Pint

Create color balance on your layouts by following the gallon, quart, pint rule of thumb. Basically all you need to do is select the color you want to be most dominant on your page. This is your "gallon" color—generally it becomes your background color.

Pick one more color for your main accent color or "quart" color. Use only half as much of this color as you use of your "gallon" color.

Then, select the third color—your "pint" color—and use just a bit of it here and there to accent the layout. Again, use only half as much of this color on the layout as you used of the "quart" color.

CONTINUED ON NEXT PAGE

This layout uses a large amount of a basic color as a background, and a slightly smaller amount of an additional color as the photo mat and stripes. A touch of an additional color is used as an accent.

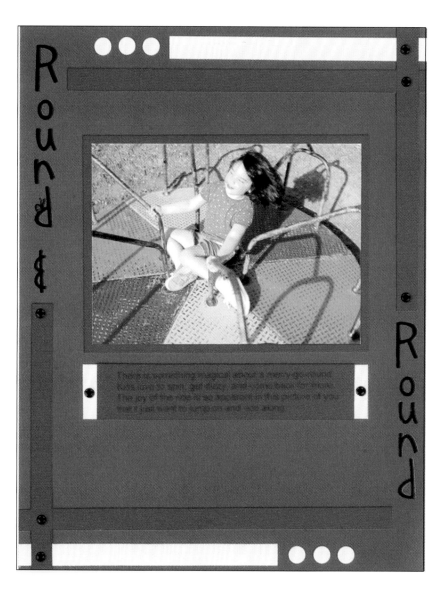

Keeping it simple is always a good rule. In scrapbooking, the photos dictate much of what you do on your pages. When it comes to selecting colors, your photos can determine which colors work best for the layout. In this layout, a bright blue monochromatic color scheme is used to highlight the subject's charming blue eyes.

Matting Essentials

Even the most basic layout can be enhanced by matting the photos, title, or journaling box in colored cardstock or paper. Mats can be used to combine photos with journaling or to link multiple photos together. Basic mats can even be embellished to create focal points for your pages.

Matting Basics

Matting a photo is simply creating a piece of cardstock that is slightly larger than the photo so that it leaves an even "frame" showing on all edges.

Mat a Photo

1. To begin, adhere your photo to a corner of a sheet of cardstock leaving equal amounts of cardstock showing on the two corner edges. Usually, ⅛" is ideal. You may choose to leave a larger amount showing, ¼" or more, to create a larger frame. You can choose to measure the ⅛" space or simply "eyeball it" for greater speed and efficiency.

2. Using a paper trimmer so that you get a nice straight cut, cut along one of the two remaining sides, once again making the cardstock ⅛" larger than the photo.

3. Finish by cutting the final edge, making it equal to the previous three sides.

4. The photo now has a perfect mat and is ready to place on a scrapbook page. This same basic technique can also be used to mat journaling boxes and embellishments.

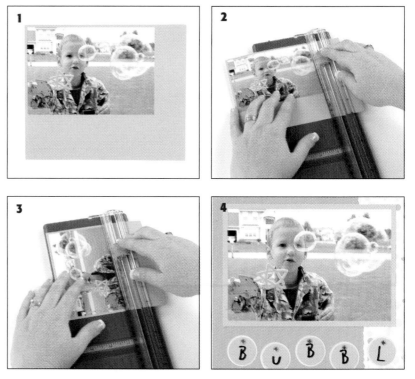

Matting photos for your scrapbook pages makes the pages look finished and professional. However, sometimes matting takes too much time to be practical for quick layouts. With this technique you can mat six photos in minutes using only one sheet of 12" × 12" cardstock.

Mats in Minutes

1. Cut the 12" × 12" cardstock in half, creating two pieces that each measure 6" × 12".

2. Cut each 6" × 12" piece into thirds, giving you a total of six pieces that measure 6" × 4".

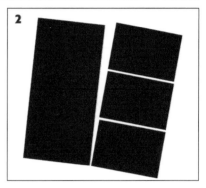

3. Trim six photos so that they each measure 5¾" × 3¾". Each photo now fits perfectly on each mat, leaving a perfect ⅛" reveal of cardstock around each photo.

4. The matted photos can now be added to your layout.

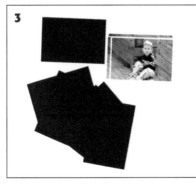

Multiple Photos on One Mat

Another quick technique for matting photos is to mat several on one strip of cardstock. This technique takes a bit of measuring, but the time it saves in the end is worth it. The finished layout uses a strip of photos across the top of the scrapbook page matted on a single piece of black cardstock.

Multi-Mats

1. Select a group of photos that work well together on one photo mat. In the layout shown here, the soccer photos give the look of a piece of sports film when they are matted all in a row.

2. Divide the width (or length) of your layout by the number of photos on the strip. Trim each photo so that they all fit on the strip.

3. Add the strip to your layout and finish the layout with other photos, journaling, and embellishments as you wish.

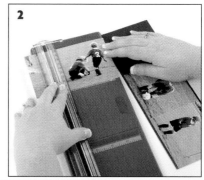

An alternate version of multiple photos on one mat is to combine a photo mat with other parts of the layout. In the example shown here, the layout shows a photo mat that includes the journaling box. Once again this technique saves time. Another advantage is that it ties different parts of the layout together to create a cohesive page.

Create the Combo

1 Print journaling on cardstock, leaving plenty of room for your photo.

2 Add photo. Trim around photo and journaling, leaving an extra inch at the bottom.

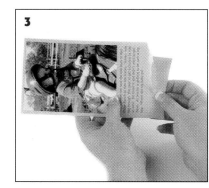

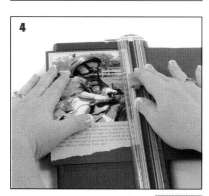

3 Tear to size across the bottom of the mat.

4 Mat the whole thing one more time in a darker color to highlight your combo mat.

Embellished Mats

You can draw attention to a particular photo in a layout by embellishing the photo mat with a decorative border. Basic techniques are shown here, but many of the advanced techniques in later chapters can also be used to embellish photo mats.

Basic Embellished Mats

1. Begin by matting a photo with ⅛" of cardstock showing on three of the sides. Trim the fourth side so that you leave a much wider border of cardstock showing. In the example shown here, the border on one side is 1" wide.

2. Embellish this wider side using punches, stickers, or letters. To begin the sample photo mat, strips of pink and green cardstock are added to the border.

3. Flower punches are added on top of the stripes in a random design.

4. To finish the border, a brightly colored mini-brad is added to the center of each flower. The completed embellished photo mat turns this photo into a focal point.

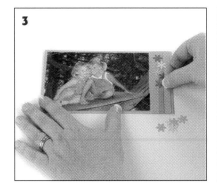

More Embellished Mats

1. Use a matted sticker and a simple strip of cardstock to decorate a photo mat.
2. Use rubber stamping to embellish the border.
3. Paper tearing in this example mimics the texture of the elephants in the photos.

6

Journaling Styles

Liven up your journaling by trying out a new technique. Whether you print on textured surfaces or hide your journaling in pockets, these ideas are sure to inspire you to use your words on your layouts.

Vellum allows the color of the paper or photos to show through behind your journaling, creating a soft, muted effect. Using your computer to print journaling on vellum can help you quickly create beautiful journaling boxes that can be placed right over a favorite photo.

Printing on Vellum

1 Print your journaling on a simple, plain vellum sheet. Usually the less expensive vellum works better in an inkjet printer. Some higher priced or printed vellum has a special coating on it that keeps the ink from drying smoothly.

If you're using an inkjet printer, try using the draft mode or the economy setting and allow the ink to dry completely before you touch the piece.

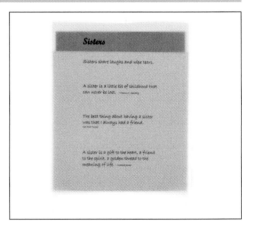

2 Trim around the printed text and attach the vellum to your photo mat using brads, nailheads, or eyelets, as shown in Chapter 10.

Transparencies are a creative way to place your journaling on top of a photo or piece of patterned paper while allowing the colors to show through completely. This allows you to add text anywhere on your scrapbook pages.

Printing on Transparencies

1 Print your quotes or journaling on transparencies that are specifically designed for your type of printer. Inkjet printer transparencies have a textured side that holds the ink in place, so be sure to place the transparency right side up in your printer.

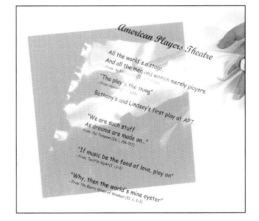

2 Allow the ink to dry completely before you trim and attach the printed transparency. You can attach the transparency to your layout or photo mat using brads, nailheads, or eyelets, as shown in Chapter 10.

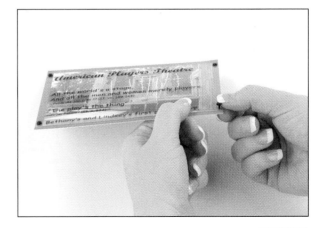

Journal on Tags

Tags are one of the most versatile embellishments in scrapbooking. You can use them to mat your photos, hold your title, or as a decorative journaling box. Follow these simple steps to print your journaling on tags.

Printing on Tags

1. Type your journaling in a text box in your favorite word processing program. Make the dimensions of this text box the size you would like your completed tag to be on your layout.

2. Print the journaling on cardstock in a color that coordinates with your layout.

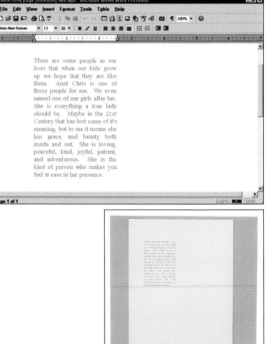

3 Trace the tag patterns from this book (see page 278) and then transfer this shape around your printed journaling. As an alternative, you could make your own tag shape with a paper trimmer as you cut out your journaling. Or you could scan the pattern from the book into your computer and print it directly onto your cardstock.

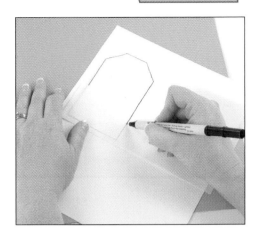

4 Cut out the tag and attach it to your layout. You may wish to punch a hole near the top of the tag for ribbon or fiber.

Photos as Journaling Pockets

Pockets are the perfect place to tuck away journaling that you want to remain a little more private. They are also a good place to hide your imperfect handwriting. A journaling pocket can be made from complicated designs, or as shown here, you can simply create one from a photo.

Turn a Photo into a Pocket

1. Select which photos on the layout will be pockets. Cut out tags following the "Journal on Tags" directions earlier in this chapter, making sure that the size of the tags fits behind the photos you have chosen. See page 278 for tag patterns.

2. Use a tacky photo tape or photo tabs to apply adhesive to the back of the photos on three sides, as close to the edge of the photo as possible. Use the tags as a guide to make sure you leave enough space so they can slide in and out behind the photo.

3. Peel off the back of the double-sided adhesive and apply the pocket directly to your layout or to a photo mat. Slip the tag into the pocket to test it for fit.

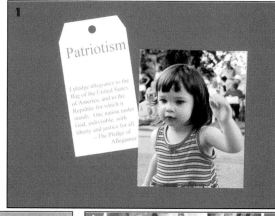

Old-fashioned embossing label makers are a fun scrapbooking tool. You can select any color cardstock and create text masterpieces. The layout here is embellished only with words.

CONTINUED ON NEXT PAGE

Emboss Words with a Label Maker

① Select cardstock that has a white core (colored outside with a white center) but a dark-colored surface. Cut the paper into ⅜" strips.

② Feed a strip, right side up, into an empty office label maker machine. As you select each letter and press the lever, the letter of your words or phrases is embossed into the paper.

③ Continue until you have embossed all the letters into the strip, then remove it from the machine. You will be able to see the raised letters on the paper, but they will not show up very well.

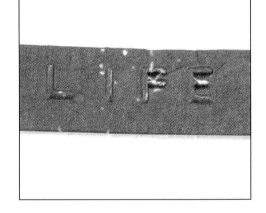

④ Use sandpaper to lightly sand the surface of the embossed letters on the strip. The sandpaper removes the color from only the letters, causing them to show up white on the background color.

Ideas for journaling holders can come from the most amazing places. These matchbook designs give you additional space on your layouts for embellishments and journaling.

CONTINUED ON NEXT PAGE

Assemble the Matchbook

1 Trace the matchbook pattern on page 280 or create your own using the measurements from the pattern. Copy this tracing onto cardstock that coordinates with your layout. The inside pages are simple rectangles that can be cut using your paper trimmer after you print your journaling on white cardstock.

2 Use a scoring tool or a scoring blade for your trimmer to score the fold lines shown on the pattern. Once scored, you can fold on each of those lines. If you don't have a score tool, simply fold carefully on the lines and crease well.

3 Insert as many pages as desired into each matchbook cover. Staple on the bottom center to hold the pages in place.

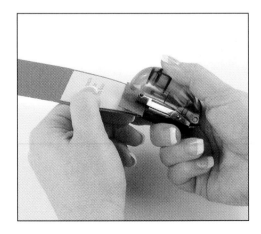

4 Embellish the matchbooks as desired and add them to your finished layout. In order to place this page in a page protector you will want to cut an opening in the protector around the matchbook to allow the reader to access the journaling.

TIP

Matchbooks designed from cardstock make excellent mini-scrapbooks. Insert several pages into the book and use them to display small photos and journaling. Embellish the cover to fit the theme of the photos. Make these little books for any gift-giving occasion. See Chapter 13 for more mini-book and theme scrapbook ideas.

File folders are not just for offices any longer. The basic shape of a classic file folder is the perfect place to insert journaling on your scrapbook pages.

Case #: 03-27-05
Suspect name: Roger

TOP SECRET

eXtreme Files

Make a File Folder for Journaling

1 Trace the file folder pattern on page 279 and transfer the pattern to colored cardstock of your choice. You could also scan this pattern into your computer and print it out directly on cardstock.

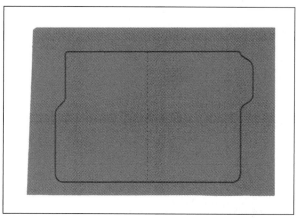

2 Use a scoring tool or a scoring blade on your trimmer to score the fold line shown on the pattern. Once scored, fold each file folder in half.

3 Embellish the outside of the file folder as desired. You could add stickers, photos, or even more journaling on the outside of the folders. Here the cover has been embellished with a sticker that says "Top Secret." Be sure to label the tab on the file folder in keeping with the office theme.

4 Add journaling to the inside of the file folder. The file folder is now ready to be added as a journaling box to your layout.

Library cards and pockets may not immediately come to mind when you think of scrapbooking. However, anything with a pocket makes an ideal, creative place to hold journaling on your layouts.

Create a Library Pocket and Journaling Card

① Transfer the library pocket pattern (see page 279) to colored cardstock that coordinates with your layout.

② Cut out the pattern and score on the fold lines.

③ Place adhesive on the tabs and press the pocket closed, making sure not to put any adhesive across the top of the pocket.

④ Print your journaling on a cardstock rectangle that will fit easily into the pocket. Mat the journaling rectangle if desired and insert it into the pocket.

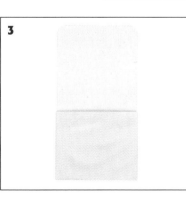

chapter 7

Designing from Page Plans

The hardest part of putting together a scrapbook page can be getting the spacing and balance just right. Page plans (or design sketches) make putting the page together quick and easy. Each plan can be adapted to fit the colors, theme, and feel of any layout.

What Is a Page Plan?

A page plan is simply a drawing of the basic parts and shapes of a scrapbook page layout. Each photo, embellishment, and journaling area has a spot on the drawing. The plan shows you the general shape of the layout, leaving the colors, style, and decorations up to your own creativity. This flexibility makes these drawings work for every type of scrapbooker.

Parts of a Page Plan

1. LAYOUT

Square or rectangle that represents the size layout you will be creating.

2. BOXES

Boxes that suggest areas for photos, journaling boxes, or large embellishments.

3. LINES

Lines that indicate places for text, or journaling.

4. EMBELLISHMENTS

Stripes, small circles, or other shapes that show where detailed embellishments may be added.

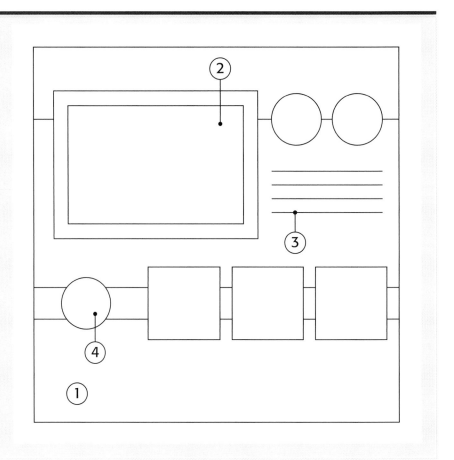

Now that you understand the parts of a page plan, turning it into a scrapbook page is simple. Using the drawing from the opposite page, you can construct this layout.

Frog Hunting

Create the Layout

1. Select a background cardstock, photos, and embellishments that coordinate with the theme or mood of the page you wish to create.

2. Decide which shapes on the plan will hold photos and crop them to fit the plan. Mat the photos if needed.

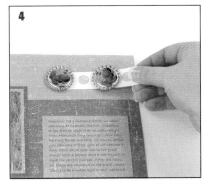

3. Print journaling and title text to fit in the places on the plan where you have decided to place your wording.

4. Insert embellishments in areas indicated to finish off the scrapbook page.

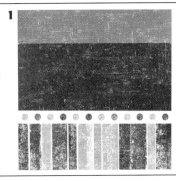

Where to Find Page Plans

Inspiration for page plan designs can be found anywhere. The graphics on clothing, magazine advertisements, and greeting cards can be sketched out to become your own collection of page plans. The layout design for some of the pages of the book you are reading right now became the inspiration for this page plan.

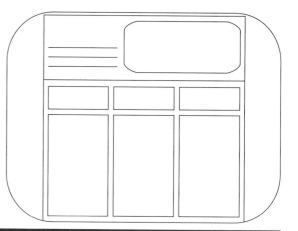

"Pretty Pampered Puppy"

"Our Little Monkey"

The beauty of page plans is that they can work with any color scheme, any page theme, and any scrapbooking style. The plan is simply the barebones graphic design for the layout. Here the designer uses the line across the page as a place to put a ribbon that coordinates with the colors of the page.

This simple page plan uses some quirky geometric shapes to add interest to the design. Notice how each designer interprets the parts of the plan and uses them to the best advantage with the theme of her scrapbook page.

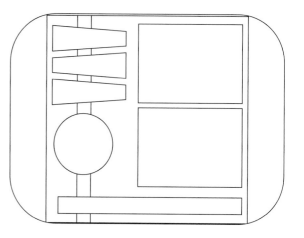

"Bath Time Fun"

"Guests, Cake, Piñata"

Here the designer uses bright colors and busy patterns to complement the fiesta theme of her scrapbook page. The same basic page plan comes to life with this vibrant color scheme.

CONTINUED ON NEXT PAGE

The more elements a page plan uses, the more complicated the design becomes. This plan uses stripes as the primary design element. Each designer uses those lines to anchor the photos on her scrapbook page. The small circles are perfect for tiny embellishments.

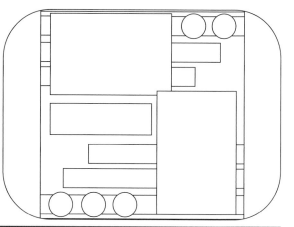

"Let It Snow"

it snow! Let it snow!

Elizabeth and Rachel are so creative. This year instead of a snowman, they wanted to make a "snow kid." They dressed it with one of their extra scarves and a old stocking cap. Then Elizabeth wanted to decorate the face. She decided for a nose that they needed a baby carrot, because a big carrot wouldn't fit their "kid."

Let it snow! Let it snow! Let it snow!

"Archery"

This elegant "Archery" scrapbook page uses antique buttons and a brass stencil as embellishments. Each part of the page has been inked before being added to the layout, creating the "aged" feel that complements the black-and-white photos.

CONTINUED ON NEXT PAGE

The most basic page plan is also the most versatile. This design simply divides the page using the rule of thirds. Each area on the layout now becomes the perfect place for a title, journaling, photos, or embellishments. Just like a perfect little black dress, this simple design can be dressed up or down to suit any theme.

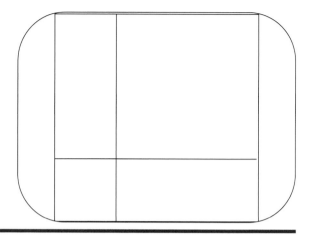

"Pretty in Pink"

"Just Keep Swimming"

In contrast to the simple, elegant feel of the "Pretty in Pink" layout, the same basic page plan is used here to create a lively and fun water-park-themed scrapbook page. The title is turned on its side so that it fits snuggly into the space divided out by the plan.

just keep swimming

Mikhail visits a waterpark
for the very first time.
Obviously, he LOVED it!
Wisconsin Dells, Wisconsin
Spring Break - 2005

8

Title Tricks

The title of a scrapbook page can set the theme for the whole layout. You can let creativity go wild when it comes to deciding which styles and techniques to use to create those titles. In this chapter, you will find everything from basic titles to unique three-dimensional lettering ideas.

Use Lettering Templates

Templates are an easy way to make titles for your pages. There are several ways to use a lettering template. Let's start with the most basic.

Basic Template Technique

1 Trace the letters using a fine-tip black journaling pen. Choose a light color of cardstock and cut it roughly to the title size that suits your layout, leaving an extra couple of inches on the end to give yourself room for letter placement. Trace each letter directly onto the cardstock.

2 Remove the template and use chalk, broad-tip pens, or colored pencils to fill in each letter.

3 Mat the title on coordinating colored cardstock to complete your title.

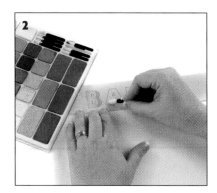

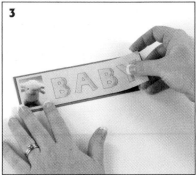

Combine Templates with Rubber Stamping

You can make a unique title for your pages by combining lettering templates with rubber stamped letters.

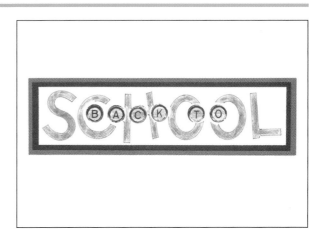

① Using a pencil, very lightly draw a straight line across the center of a strip of cardstock.

② On the line, stamp all but the last word of your title.

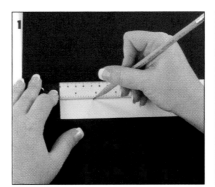
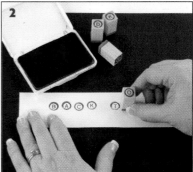

③ Trace the last word of the title using a lettering template over the top of the stamped letters, being careful to stop your pen whenever it intersects with the rubber stamped words.

④ Erase your initial pencil line. Fill in the traced letters with colored pencils and mat on colored cardstock to complete your title.

CONTINUED ON NEXT PAGE

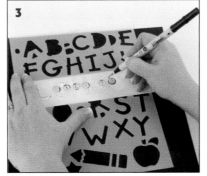

Trace and Cut Letters from a Template

Templates also allow you to create letters from any color of cardstock you choose for your layout. A few simple steps can help you get nice-looking letters each time.

① Select the color of cardstock you wish to use for your title. Turn this piece of cardstock over. Flip your template over also and lay it on the back of the cardstock. By doing all of the tracing on the back of the cardstock, you will not need to erase any lines later.

② Trace each letter lightly in pencil. Placement does not matter because you will be cutting each one out. You may wish to line up the template so that you conserve as much cardstock as possible.

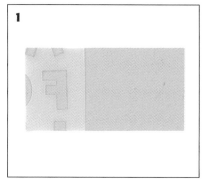

③ Cut out each letter. When cutting letters with inside pieces such as a capital "A," simply cut straight through to the center and finish cutting out the piece. When you adhere the letter to your layout you will not even notice the cut line.

④ Adhere the cut letters to a basic mat to complete your title. See "Matting Basics" in Chapter 5.

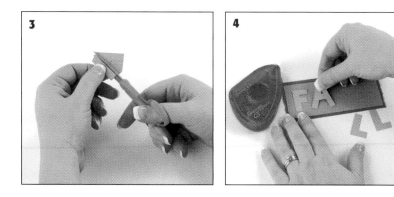

Layered Letter with Templates

Once you know the simple steps for cutting letters from card-stock using templates, you can add to that technique by making beautiful layered letters. The layers of cardstock can be used to accent any page theme and really make your titles stand out.

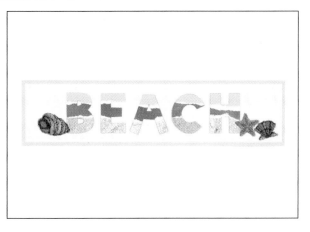

① Choose coordinating colors or prints of cardstock or even pattered paper. In the sample shown here, a strip of light blue cardstock is combined with "water" and "sand" prints of paper. Create a strip using these colors of paper that shows each one as much or as little as you desire, making sure they are close enough to each other so that they all appear on each letter traced from your template.

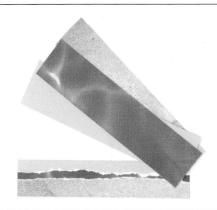

② Make sure that the strips of paper are completely adhered together or to a base of colored cardstock. When you begin cutting out letters, any little parts that are not stuck down will fall off. Use a pencil to lightly trace each letter of your title.

③ Cut out the letters and adhere to a background of cardstock to complete your title. Embellishments such as stickers may be added to finish the look.

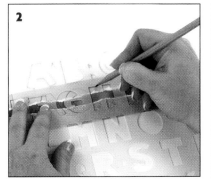

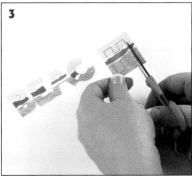

Sticker Letters

Stickers are a quick and easy way to create a page title. Sometimes getting them lined up just right or running out of a particular letter can be a challenge, but these simple steps can help you make them perfect every time.

Align Sticker Letters

1. Decide where on your layout you would like to place the title. If the title needs to be perfectly straight, you may get frustrated as you attempt to adhere each letter. Instead, find a piece of already used sticker backing sheet or even a strip of tape runner backing.

2. Line up each letter of the title across this backing sheet just as you would like them to appear on your page. Allow only a tiny bit of the bottom of each letter to adhere to the backing sheet; the tops of the letters should be placed so that they stick out above the backing.

3. When all of the letters are in place, move the backing sheet over your layout, and press the tops of all of the letter stickers in place.

4. Carefully roll the backing sheet out from behind the bottoms of the letters and then press the letters into place.

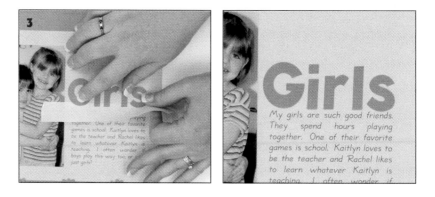

Occasionally when using sticker letters, you may find that the letter you need has already been used. No need to panic; many letters can be transformed into other letters with just a quick snip of your scissors.

Sticker Letter Transformation

1 To replace the letter A, for example, find a letter on your sticker letter sheet that has a similar shape such as a V. Use another letter that has a straight section, such as U, to cut the piece that goes across the center of the new A.

2 Simply use a sharp pair of scissors to trim the excess away to turn an E into an F or an L into an I. Trimming away the excess also allows an X to become a Y, an R to become a P, a Q to become an O, and an H to become an I.

3 Lowercase letters d, h, and m can become l, n, and n, respectively. Two lowercase v's put together become a w.

1

$$V \circlearrowleft A + U = A$$

2

$E \times E = F$	$R \times R = P$
$L \times L = I$	$Q \times Q = O$
$X \times X = Y$	$H \times H = I$

3

$d \times d = l$	$m \times m = n$
$h \times h = n$	$v + v = w$

4 Lowercase letters can be flipped so that p becomes d, q becomes b, and u becomes n (or vice versa).

4

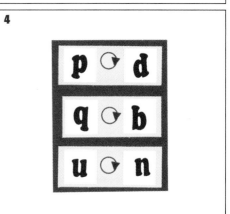

p	$\circlearrowright$	d
q	$\circlearrowright$	b
u	$\circlearrowright$	n

Scrapbookers can choose from a variety of styles and sizes of die-cutting machines. Each machine and set of letter dies fall into a different price range. Whether you decide to purchase your own or use the machine at your local scrapbook store, these simple techniques can help you make creative titles for your pages.

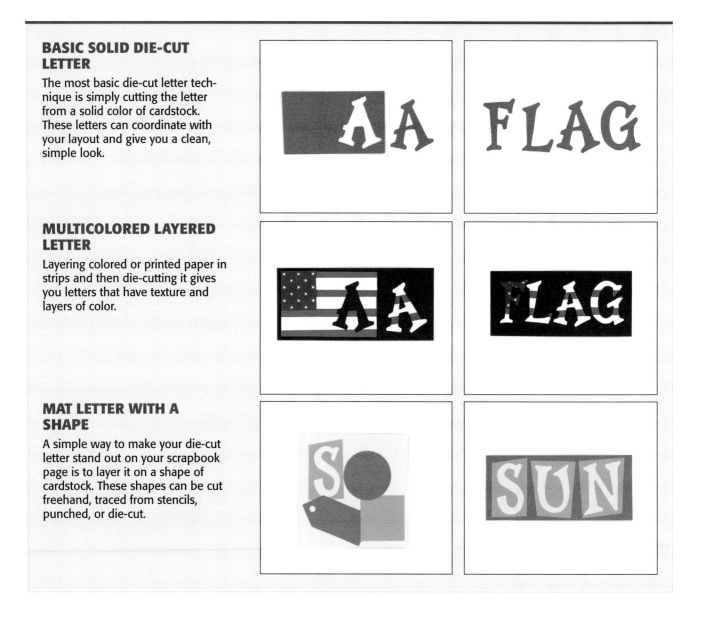

BASIC SOLID DIE-CUT LETTER

The most basic die-cut letter technique is simply cutting the letter from a solid color of cardstock. These letters can coordinate with your layout and give you a clean, simple look.

MULTICOLORED LAYERED LETTER

Layering colored or printed paper in strips and then die-cutting it gives you letters that have texture and layers of color.

MAT LETTER WITH A SHAPE

A simple way to make your die-cut letter stand out on your scrapbook page is to layer it on a shape of cardstock. These shapes can be cut freehand, traced from stencils, punched, or die-cut.

SHADOW LETTERS

Die-cutting letters from two contrasting colors or prints allows you to add a "shadow" to give your letters depth.

LETTERS WITH POP

Double-sided foam adhesive is used to "pop" items off your scrapbook page. Place this adhesive foam on the back of your die-cut letters so that they appear to leap from the layout.

INVERSE DIE-CUT LETTERS

When you cut a letter from cardstock, the leftover piece shows the "inverse" of the letter. Use this technique to allow the background color to show through the letters in your title.

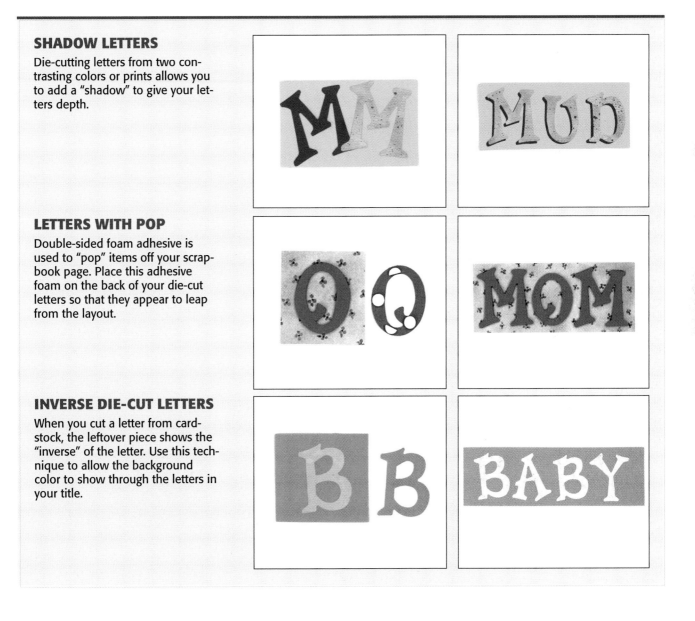

Die-Cut Shaker Titles

Make die-cut titles three-dimensional by creating these fun shaker titles. Your pages come to life when the titles have movement and depth.

Making a Shaker

1. Layer the paper and strips to make layered die-cut letters. Die-cut the letters needed for your title.

2. Die-cut the letters from coordinating color foam.

3. Adhere the foam letters to the title mat. Select one or more letters to fill with beads and cover all of the foam letters with the layered die-cut letters.

4. Cut a small piece of plastic page protector to size so that it seals in the beads in your title letter. Adhere this piece of plastic in place. Once sealed, finish the last letter by adding the layered die-cut letter on top.

In the layout shown here, the shaker title accents the theme of the page. The moving beads draw attention to the quick steps of the Irish dancing. By changing the colors of the layered die-cut letters and the seed beads, this technique could be used for a scrapbook page based on any theme.

Tag Shaker Titles

The same techniques used to make shaker titles can be used to construct the opposite style of a die-cut title—a tag shaker. With these titles, the entire letter can be filled with beads, glitter, sand, or other tiny embellishments.

Making a Tag Shaker

1. Die-cut four tags for each letter in your title: one cut from base cardstock, one from craft foam, one from a clear plastic page protector, and one from patterned paper.

2. Take the foam tag and the patterned paper tag and die-cut a letter from your title for each of them.

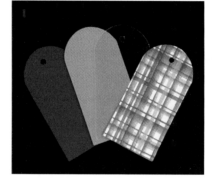
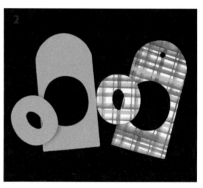

3. Adhere the foam to the cardstock base tag using liquid, permanent glue. Fill the letter shape with seed beads, and adhere the clear plastic tag over the foam base to seal in the beads.

4. Add the final tag—patterned paper—on top of the shaker to complete the letter.

5. Repeat steps 1–4 for each letter in the title.

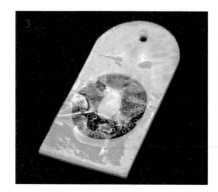
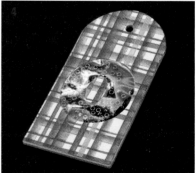

The layout shown here uses shaker tags to spell out "TOYS." The letters have been strung on red ribbon to make it appear that the tags are "hanging" on the page.

Painted Chipboard Titles

Chipboard is compressed cardboard that can be found on the back of paper packs. Cutting this material into blocks or die-cutting it into letters and shapes allows you to make tiles and letters for title techniques.

Painted Tile Titles

1. Cut pieces of chipboard into shapes that suit your title. For this "Bath" title the chipboard has been punched into circles.

2. Paint each piece with a coat of acrylic paint and allow them to dry completely. In this example, blue paint and clear glitter paint were mixed to give the shapes extra sparkle like bubbles.

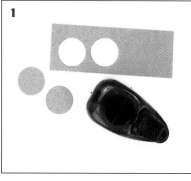
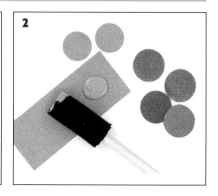

3. When the shapes are dry, press rub-on letters in place with a craft stick to add a letter to each shape.

4. To add extra shine and dimension to the letters, spray them with clear-coat acrylic spray and allow to dry completely. Add the letters to your mat to complete your title.

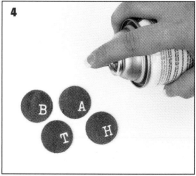

On this page, the chipboard is cut into funky rectangles, painted, and then rubber-stamped with each letter in the title. Chipboard is also die-cut into flower shapes, painted, and sprayed with clear-coat acrylic to further embellish the scrapbook layout.

Rubber Stamping Titles

Stamping and scrapbooking are crafts that work exceptionally well together. Good rubber stamps can be a significant investment, so choose designs that you can use again and again, such as letter stamps. Letter stamps are fabulous for scrapbook page titles.

Rubber Stamping Basics

1. Select an ink pad that is permanent, acid-free, and fade-resistant in a color that coordinates with your layout. Press a rubber or foam stamp letter on the stamp pad firmly. Tap it on the pad a couple of times to be sure the whole image is inked.

2. Press the inked stamp on the paper where desired. Continue with the rest of the letters in the title. Allow to dry completely before you add photos or embellishments to the layout.

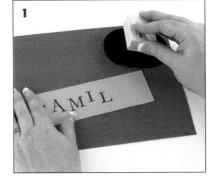

3. Lining up the letters can sometimes be a challenge when you are stamping one letter at a time. Instead, you could purposely tilt each letter slightly to make your title fun and funky (a). Or, you could stamp each letter individually and cut it out in a rectangle to make letter tiles (b).

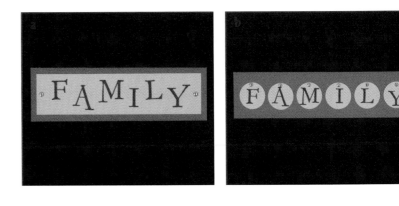

Bleached Titles

Some colored cardstock allows you to lighten the color with bleach. Before using this technique, experiment a little with your paper of choice to see how it responds to a dab of bleach. If the color lightens nicely, you know that you have a winner.

Bleaching a Title

① This process is best completed in a well-ventilated area. Select paper that you have pre-tested and has responded well to the bleaching process. Place a folded piece of paper towel on a plate and wet it with bleach, just until the whole towel is damp. This becomes your stamp pad. Press a rubber or foam stamp letter into the paper towel lightly, making sure the entire letter comes in contact with the bleach.

② Press the wet stamp on the paper where desired. Continue with the rest of the letters in the title. Allow to dry completely before you add photos or embellishments to the layout. To wash off your stamps, simply rinse them with clean water and let dry.

Metal Lettering

Letters for scrapbook titles can be found on brads, eyelets, and other metal embellishments. Mixing these letters together can give you a fun and creative title technique.

Mixing Metal Letters

1 Decide on one word in your title that you wish to make out of metal. Select the letters you need to complete this word from a variety of metal letter sources.

2 Attach each letter to the title using a variety of techniques—brads, eyelets, fibers, etc. (See Chapter 10 for help setting brads and eyelets.)

3 Complete by matting the title and adding it to your layout.

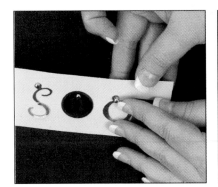

Brad Rub-On Lettering

Brass brads are simple to use and make one of the easiest embellishments. By adding letters to brads, you create a dimensional design for your pages that can also act as the title or part of the journaling.

Adding Letters to Brads

1. Select the word or phrase you wish to make out of brads. Insert into a piece of cardstock the number of brads that equal the number of letters in your title.

2. Cut out the rub-on letters, leaving as much room as possible on each side to give you something to hold on to as you rub the letters onto the brads. Add the letters one at a time to the tops of the brads.

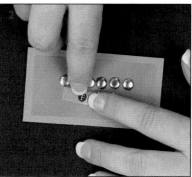

3. Continue until all title letters have been added to the brads. The title shown here uses special rub-on letters made for brads.

4. You can also find small rub-on letters at office supply stores that work well on brads—an example "e" is shown here.

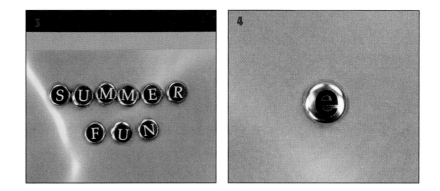

Clay Letters

Crafters have been using polymer clay for jewelry making, sculpting, and more for years. Both this clay and air-dry paper clay can be used to make three-dimensional letters for scrapbook page titles.

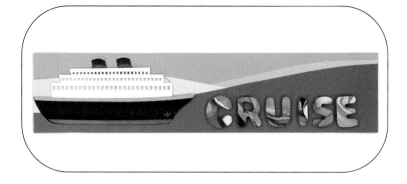

Making Clay Letters

1. To get a variegated color letter, mix two or more shades of clay together. To do this, simply take a tablespoon size of each of the two colors and twist and roll them until you have achieved the desired blend. Here we have mixed blue and white polymer clay.

2. Use a small rolling pin or a piece of wooden dowel to roll the clay out to an even ¼-inch thickness.

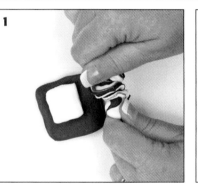

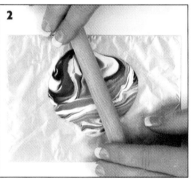

3. Press cookie-cutter type letter cutters into the clay for each letter needed for the title. Bake the letters on a cookie sheet following manufacturer's directions.

   Remove from the oven and let cool. If using air-dry clay, let the clay dry as directed on the package before using on your layout.

4. Adhere the letters to your cardstock title mat with adhesive dots or liquid glue to complete your title.

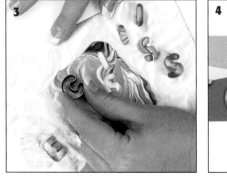

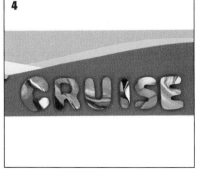

Stencil Paste Letters

Acid-free stencil paste makes letters that have both dimension and texture. The paste dries to an almost rubbery consistency so it will not break, crack, or flake off of your pages. This fun technique is a quick way to give your pages a really unique look.

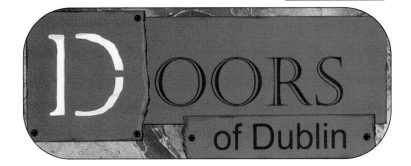

Using Spackle Paste for Letters

① Select stencil paste that is acid-free and made for paper crafts. You will also need a lettering stencil and a plastic putty knife.

② Adhere scrap cardstock to cover the letters adjacent to the letter you are working with. Line the stencil up over the piece of cardstock you wish to use for your title or monogram (single letter). Using the putty knife, spread an even layer of paste over the letter.

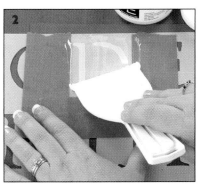

③ Carefully lift the stencil off of the background cardstock, leaving just the shape of the letter in stencil paste behind. Allow to dry for two or three hours.

④ Adhere the completed letter on cardstock to your layout or title mat. At this point you may choose to further embellish the letter with chalk, stamping ink, or paint. In the sample shown here, the ink has been lightly brushed with a fingertip over the letter to bring out the texture of the letter.

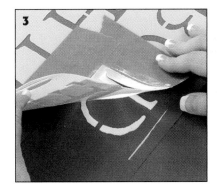
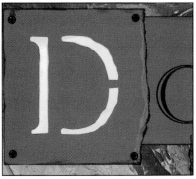

Die-Cutting Fabric, Cork, and More

Many die-cut machines can cut a variety of materials. Discovering just what you can cut into letters gives your titles even more texture and adds more fun to your layouts.

CORK

You can purchase cork in sheets from your local craft store. These sheets work with most dies and make letters that are lightweight with plenty of texture and dimension.

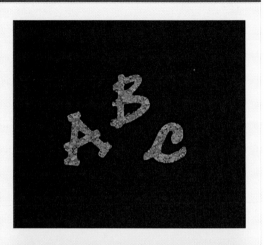

FABRIC AND FELT

Almost any type of fabric can be cut in a die-cut machine. The sample shown here uses some denim scraps. The fuzzy felt letters add texture to your pages.

HVAC TAPE

Metal embellishments are extremely popular in scrapbooking. Sometimes the thickness and weight of these items can deter crafters. Die-cutting cardstock that is covered with a piece of aluminum tape (found at the hardware store) creates a faux metal title.

FOAM

Craft foam is easy to cut with a die-cut machine and makes fun three-dimensional lettering for titles. Foam comes in a variety of colors as well as fun prints like zebra stripe and tie-dye.

FAQ

How do I know what materials can be cut with my die-cut machine?
Always check the manufacturer's instructions that came with the machine to see a list of materials that have been tested with the machine and its dies. You can damage your die-cut equipment if you try to cut items that are too thick or dense for the dies to cut through. If you no longer have the instructions that came with your machine, check the manufacturer's Web site.

9

Paper Techniques

Paper is the most basic supply used in scrapbooking. With a few simple techniques, you can turn plain pieces of cardstock into creative works of art.

Paper tearing is quicker and has more texture than simply cutting paper with a trimmer. It requires no special tools or skills. A few pointers can help you get your paper tearing just right.

Basic Tearing Techniques

Hold the part of the cardstock you wish to keep in your dominant hand (that is, if you are right-handed, hold it in your right hand). Slowly tear the paper toward you. The piece you are keeping will have a nice fuzzy edge. Continue down the piece slowly using your thumbs to guide the tear.

If you are using solid cardstock that has even color all the way through, the tear simply adds rough texture (a).

Cardstock or patterned paper with a white core shows as a white edge when torn. This white edge can be inked, chalked, or used as is in your design (b).

On this scrapbook page, the entire background is made up of torn paper. The page started with a solid piece of blue printed cardstock as a background; each coordinating color was torn and added in layers.

Geometric Borders

Paper punched into basic geometric shapes can have a huge impact on the overall design of your pages. The shapes can be arranged in a border stripe or divided up to fill in blank space.

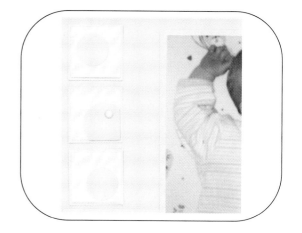

Geo Squares

Use punches to make shapes in coordinating colors to go with your layout. Choose one color and shape to be the background for each design. In this example, the background is a square.

Layer the shapes as desired to decorate the squares. Allow some of the shapes to extend off the edge of the bottom shape. Use scissors to trim the shape even with the edge of the base.

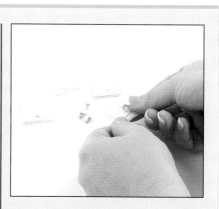

Mat each finished square and add an embellishment such as an eyelet or brad to complete the shape. Add these squares to your layout in a line to create a border.

These geometric decorated squares do not have to be placed all in a row. Instead, you can use them to add interest in open spaces of your layout. On this layout, squares are used to accent the photo and fill space on the bottom of the page.

Sleeping Steven

Steven mommy thinks you are adorable especially when you sleep. I enjoy just watching you and admiring your beauty. You have the tiniest little hands. and I love the hands above the head pose. It is so tempting to reach into your cradle to feel your fuzzy head. but you never want to wake a sleeping baby. However it good to take the time to admire how cute they are.

Serendipity Squares

Serendipity means "happy accident." Mix up your scraps of paper and you will be pleasantly surprised with beautiful serendipity squares that you can use to decorate your pages.

Make the Squares

1. Start with a large sheet of cardstock—6" × 6" is large enough. Begin layering torn pieces of cardstock onto this background sheet. Make sure that each piece you add is completely glued down to the background sheet.

2. Further embellish the background sheet by adding rubber stamping. Simply stamp a design in a random pattern all over the piece. Be sure to turn the stamp and also stamp over the edge occasionally.

3 When you are happy with the coverage of the background cardstock, use your trimmer to cut it into squares. These can be any size you want—1½" is a good choice for your first project. Mat each of these squares in a coordinating color of cardstock.

4 Finish by adding the squares to your layout. They can be placed in a row to form a border or they can be scattered over the page to fill in blank spaces. They look best in groupings of two or three squares each.

Paper generally is the flat part of your scrapbook pages. By sanding, crumpling, and ironing your cardstock you can give it texture and dimension.

SANDING

Any cardstock can be sanded to give it texture. Cardstock or papers with a white core, however, have the most dramatic transformation when sanded. The white shows through the colored layer, making the paper look aged and weathered. Manufacturers have even made sanding blocks like the one shown here to protect scrapbookers' manicures.

CRUMPLING

Cardstock has a fabulous textured surface when it has been crumpled and then flattened back out. To make crumpling both easier and more effective, spray the surface with a light mist of water first. Allow the water to soak in for just a minute and then crumple as usual. When the paper is damp, it will give you a more even texture throughout the surface.

IRONING

Take crumpling up a notch by ironing the crumpled cardstock. Ironing the paper helps it dry quickly and gives it a unique texture. Pre-heat the iron on its "cotton" heat setting. Keep the iron moving over the paper, to prevent scorching it. When ironed, all of the folds from crumpling become fine, permanent creases, giving the paper a surface that resembles leather.

Combine crumpling, tearing, sanding, and ironing on one layout for a rustic textured feel. The layout shown here uses colors that accent the photos while the paper techniques give the page some dimension.

When people find out that we had three girls and then a boy they often ask, "Is having a boy different?" In the beginning I would say not really, but now that he is two Steven is all boy. He loves "boy" toys, cars, trucks, trains and balls. He has a sound effect for everything. He climbs everywhere, and he stomps when he walks. It is so fun to see him develop into our little boy.

BOY TOYS

Ink pads are not just for rubber stamping any more. Scrapbookers use ink techniques to add interest to cardstock and aging to patterned papers.

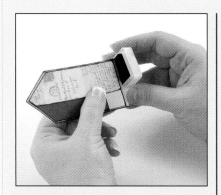

DIRECT TO PAPER

To accent the edges of cardstock as shown on this tag, hold the ink pad perpendicularly to the edge of the paper and lightly brush the pad down its length. Continue brushing the pad along the edge of the paper all the way around each piece you wish to highlight. On this tag, each piece was inked before it was added to the tag, and, the final step is to ink the edges of the tag itself.

RUB ON INK

Age your papers or cardstocks by rubbing ink into the paper to give it a "tea stain" or old paper look. Simply dab a make-up sponge onto the ink pad and then rub the sponge over the paper. Start light and add more layers of ink until you have the desired shade. The more you add the older and more distressed the paper appears.

ADD STRIPES

You can add stripes of color to cardstock by using a multicolor ink pad. Slide the ink pad across the paper, being sure to follow the direction of the stripes on the pad. The tag shown here can now be used as a mat for journaling or other embellishments on a scrapbook page.

Chalk can quickly become a scrapbooker's best friend. Much more subtle than ink, chalk can be used to accent edges and highlight sections of embellishments, journaling, and papers.

Chalks come in a variety of packaging and sizes. You can get them in individual squares, pie-shaped triangles, or even in pencils.

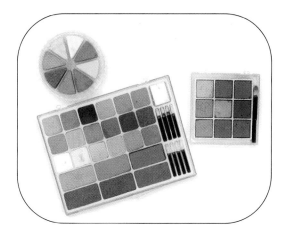

Chalks adhere best to paper when it has some texture to grab on to. It is perfect for highlighting a torn cardstock edge.

Chalk is ideal for highlighting words in a paragraph of journaling. Select the most important words, outline them with a fine-tip pen, and lightly chalk.

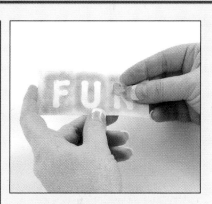

For a subtle title effect, you can chalk around die-cut letters and then remove them to leave a chalk shadow. Hold the cardstock letter in place and rub chalk around it with a cotton swab until the color reaches the desired darkness.

Paper piecing is the art of creating pictures with paper. Each piece is cut out and layered to make the finished project. Although the process can be time-consuming, the finished look can make a scrapbook page extra special.

Make the Giraffe

1. The first step in paper piecing is transferring the pattern to your choice of colored cardstock. See page 281 for the pattern. To begin, lay a piece of tracing paper or vellum over the top of the pattern and trace.

2. Roughly cut out each piece from the tracing paper or vellum. Do not cut directly on the lines, but rather quickly cut around the traced pattern, simply separating each piece. If the pattern has a lot of pieces, you may wish to label each one as you trace it.

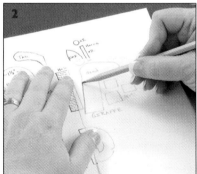

3 Flip the piece of tracing paper over and use some removable (or a tiny bit of permanent) adhesive to attach the traced pattern to the cardstock (a). By turning the piece over before you attach it, any damage done by the glue is on the back of the finished cardstock piece. Now cut out each piece directly on the lines, which you can see through the tracing paper (b).

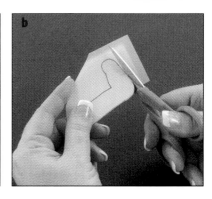

4 In this pattern, the giraffe's mane has some special instructions. First transfer the pattern and cut out the cardstock into the long rectangle of the mane.

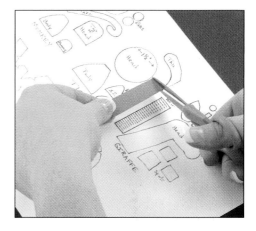

5 Next, cut three-fourths of the way through the paper over and over again, as close together as possible—leaving a scant ⅛" strip between each cut (a). Continue down the entire rectangle (b).

CONTINUED ON NEXT PAGE

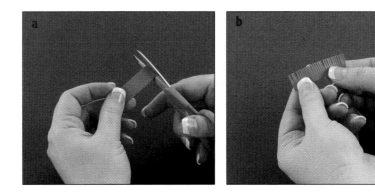

6. Once all the lines have been cut, start again at the beginning of the strip and snip out every other piece (a). This leaves the rectangle looking like a comb, or a giraffe's mane (b).

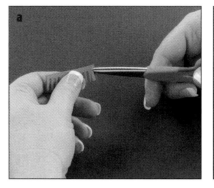
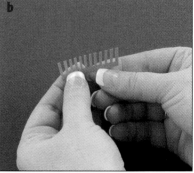

7. Put the pieces together as shown in the finished example. Adhere them to matted rectangles that coordinate with the scrapbook page.

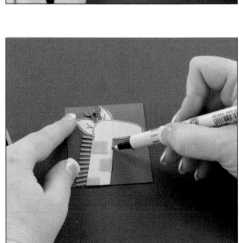

8. Use a black fine-tip journaling pen to outline each piece. Also, use this pen to add features to each animal. For the giraffe, add spirals on the tips of the horns, an eye and eyebrow, a spiral nostril, and a slight smile.

9 Complete the piece with just a touch of chalk (a). Use a cotton swab to add pink chalk to the inside of the giraffe's ears and the cheek (b).

10 Follow the same basic steps used to make the giraffe, to complete the tiger and the monkey. The tiger's stripes are added with a black fine-tip pen. If desired, outline each animal's rectangle with dashes and dots.

Our family has always loved the zoo. The kids love the animals and Doug and I just love taking a walk as a family. The best part about The Binder Park Zoo is that you can hand feed the giraffes.

Sewing on Paper

You can use your sewing machine to stitch on your scrapbook pages. It's true! This easy technique can be used to create beautiful pages in minutes.

Getting Started Stitching

1. Trim cardstock or paper pieces as desired and tack them down on your layout with small bits of adhesive (a). Be careful to apply adhesive only in the center of the pieces, keeping it away from where you will be stitching. Set the stitch length on your sewing machine to a long setting so that the holes will be farther apart as you stitch through the paper (b).

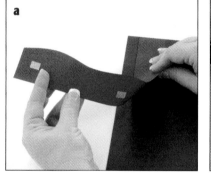

2. Choose either a straight or zig-zag stitch and carefully sew along the seams on your paper (a). Do not back up over the same spot to "tie-off" the end or you may tear the paper. Finish by trimming off the threads (b). Add photos and embellishments to complete the layout.

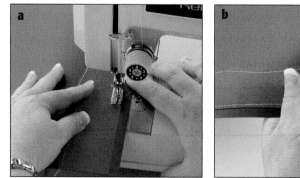
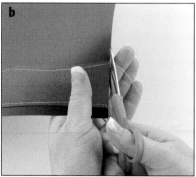

On this layout, the top and bottom borders are stitched to the page. This takes just minutes to complete and gives the page a "finished" feel. The flower embellishments on this page, purchased from the sewing section at a craft store, complement the sewing.

Sewn Vellum Journaling Boxes

Machine stitching on paper is so easy and makes a great scrapbook technique. When you take that technique one step further you can create elegant sewn vellum journaling boxes for your pages.

> Lindsey loved preschool from the very first day! Her teacher, Mrs. Hollander, made the kids feel right at home in the classroom, which was filled with fun things to explore.
>
> Fall 2001

Stitching the Journaling Box

1. Print journaling, a poem, or a quote on vellum and trim leaving ½" all the way around for a border.

2. Cut a mat for the vellum from double-sided, printed paper. Make the mat ⅜" larger than the vellum on all four sides.

3. Place some flat decorative items, such as plastic confetti, between the vellum and the paper, and fold the edges of the paper over the vellum.

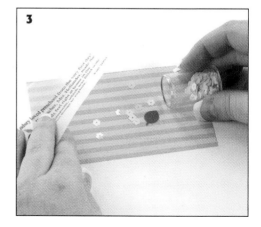

4. To get perfect mitered corners, fold each corner in toward the center of the vellum box and crease. Open the corner and trim with scissor just outside of the creased line.

5. Carefully stitch around all four sides of the box with your sewing machine. Be sure that you select a long stitch length and go slowly around each corner.

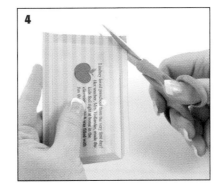

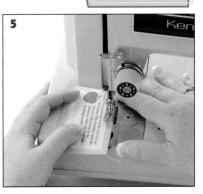

Vellum 3-D Flowers

These lovely three-dimensional flowers are just plain fun to make. They are beautiful scrapbook page embellishments, but would also look great on wrapped gifts, cards, or other paper crafts.

Make the Flowers

1. Use a large flower punch to punch flower shapes out of a sheet of vellum.

2. Carefully transfer a Pop-Up GlueDot™ to the center of each flower so that the curved side of the dot is upright, creating a large dome of sticky glue in the center of each flower.

3. Press the sticky center of each flower into a pile of small seed beads. Repeat as needed until the dot of adhesive is completely covered in beads.

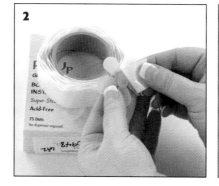

A vellum envelope is the perfect place to store memorabilia on your scrapbook page. The vellum protects the contents while allowing you to see through it to know what is inside. Consider this technique when you want to add tickets, room keys, or other flat mementos to your pages.

Create an Envelope

1 Using an embossing stylus or pen cap, trace the pattern for the envelope onto the vellum. See page 278 for the pattern. This will create a white line that you won't have to worry about erasing later.

2 Cut out the envelope and crease on the fold lines.

3 Use a large circle punch to create a notch in the front of the pocket. Turn the circle punch upside down so you can see exactly where you are punching.

4 Fold and glue down the tabs to finish the envelope. Be sure to glue the flaps to the back of the envelope and not inside of it; that way they will not "catch" every time you insert the memorabilia into the pocket.

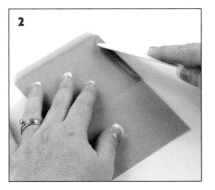

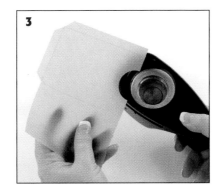

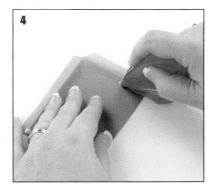

chapter **10**

Three-Dimensional Embellishments

Scrapbooking is not just about flat surfaces. Everything from silk flowers to zippers can be included on your pages. Expand your creativity with three-dimensional techniques on your next scrapbook page layout.

Eyelets

Eyelets are tiny grommets. They come in a wide variety of shapes and colors, but the one thing they all have in common is that you need tools to "set" them. The basic tools and steps for setting an eyelet are shown here.

Set an Eyelet

① Use an "anywhere hole punch" to punch a hole the size of the shank of your eyelet in the cardstock. Place a cutting mat under the cardstock and hold the punching tool in place where you wish to make the hole.

② Strike the top of the tool once or twice to punch a hole through the paper.

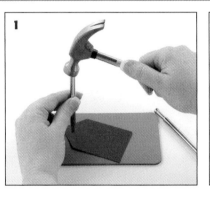

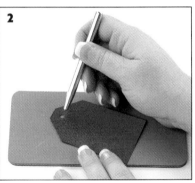

③ Insert your eyelet through the hole and hold it carefully in place as you turn the paper over.

④ Switch to an eyelet-setting tool. Place this tool with the tip balanced in the center of the back of the eyelet, and hit it with a hammer twice. This will roll or split the back of the eyelet to lock it in place.

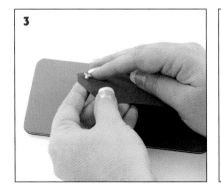

An eyelet can hold down the corner of a photo mat to create a simple three-dimensional embellishment. Once the eyelet is in place, other tiny decorations can hang from the new hole. This 6" × 6" scrapbook page is an example of this technique.

Make the Photo Mat

1 Mat the photo on printed paper, trimming the upper right corner of the photo slightly so that the corner is not quite so thick.

2 Flip the matted photo over and decorate the corner of the paper behind where you trimmed the corner of the photo. Here we added blue printed paper and a piece of printed transparency.

3 Turn the photo mat back over and fold the corner to the front gently, trying to roll the corner rather than crease it. Set an eyelet in the corner to hold it in place.

4 Tie a charm to a piece of floss. Thread the floss through the hole and tape it on the back of the mat, allowing the charm to hang freely on the front of the photo.

Brads

Brads are extremely popular in scrap-booking not only because they come in a huge variety of colors, sizes, and shapes, but also because they are very easy to use.

Insert a Brad

1. The only tools you need to set a brad are a regular office push-pin and an upside-down mouse pad.

2. To begin, place the area you wish to add a brad to on top of the upside-down mouse pad. Use the push-pin to poke a hole exactly where you wish to place the brad. The mouse pad provides a surface that supports the paper while allowing the pin to penetrate.

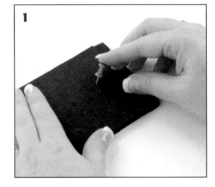

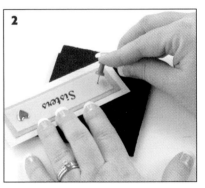

3. Press the brad into the hole and open the two prongs on the back to hold it in place (a). The hole made by the push-pin is perfect for mini-brads. If the brad prongs are larger than the hole you may need to poke another one right next to it to enlarge the hole (b).

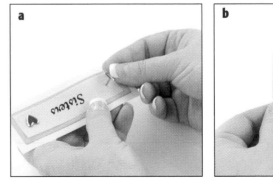

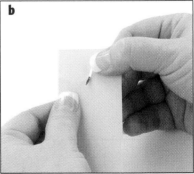

Brads are excellent attachments for holding items to your pages. They are ideal for vellum and transparencies. Brads by themselves, however, can decorate pages in the same way that cuff links accent a tuxedo shirt. On the layout shown here, sets of three brads are used in different areas of the page simply as accents.

Slide Mounts

Slide mounts are ideal lightweight frames for scrapbook pages. You can frame small photos, words, or other embellishments. On the layout shown here, paper slide mounts are simply used to frame charms that match the theme of the layout.

Slide mounts have been used in the photography industry for decades. These small shapes are photo-safe and perfect for scrapbooking. Of course, before you use them on your pages you may wish to decorate them, so here are several ideas for embellishing slide mounts.

Slide mounts come in both a thick paper cardboard and plastic. Spray-painting slide mounts with metallic spray paint is a quick and easy way to make lightweight, faux metal page embellishments.

Covering slide mounts in patterned paper allows you to coordinate them with any layout. Simply trace the shape on the back of the slide mount and cut out the paper before you adhere it to the top of the mount.

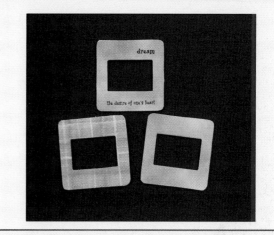

Double-sided, high-tack tape allows you to cover slide mounts in beads, glitter, or even sand. Simply cover the slide mount in the tape and dip it into a bowl of the beads or other material to cover.

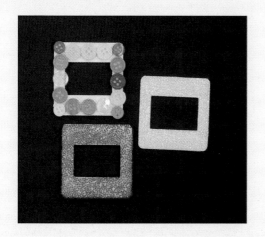

You can paint slide mounts with acrylic craft paint to change the color. You can then rubber-stamp or rub-on designs or words to further embellish the mounts.

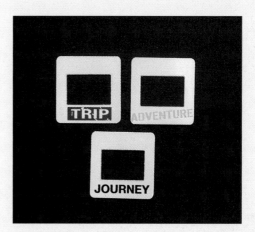

Silk Flowers

Once you have been scrapbooking for a little while you will start to come up with ideas for things that could embellish your pages. Silk flowers are lightweight, soft, and come in beautiful colors, making them the perfect page decoration.

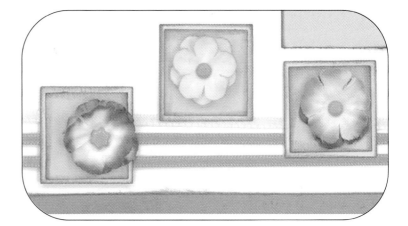

Make a Flower

1 Start by removing the fabric flower part from any plastic on the stem. Using the color of the flower as a guide, select a round or decorative brad that would work nicely with the flower.

2 Punch or cut squares big enough to hold the flowers on your layout. You may wish to ink or chalk the edges of these squares.

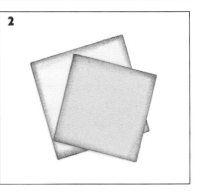

3 Layer two or more flowers on top of one another and position them on the cardstock square. Use a push-pin to poke a hole in the middle of the flowers through the cardstock and add the brad to the center to hold the flowers in place.

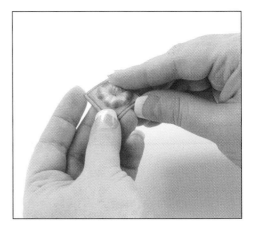

Once you have completed several silk flower squares, you can add them to your layout. These flowers give the page a three-dimensional touch of femininity while adding lovely texture and color. On the layout shown here, the pretty-in-pink baby doll photos are accented by the pink flower squares.

Dear Rachel,

How many great women learned to be GREAT by playing with BABY DOLLS ? Baby dolls teach you to pretend, imagine, believe, dream, and love, which will take you far in life.

Never let anything stand in the way of your DREAMS . Just IMAGINE you can be anything you want to be and go for it. BELIEVE to the end. PRETEND the impossible until it is possible. HUG with all your MIGHT , and LOVE with your HEART . Hold on tight and you will go far.

Love, Mom

Fibers

Another simple way to add dimension and texture to your scrapbook pages is by adding a bit of ribbon, yarn, floss, or raffia. In scrapbooking, these types of embellishments are often categorized as "fibers."

RIBBON

Ribbon is a favorite among scrapbookers. It comes in a huge range of colors, widths, and textures. You can add quick stripes to a page or staple bits of ribbon to the edge of a photo mat for a funky embellishment.

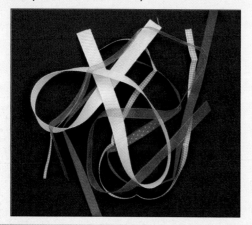

FLOSS

Floss comes in two categories: cotton floss traditionally used by needle crafters and paper floss used in general crafting. Floss can be used to stitch on your layouts or to tie items through eyelets or around brads.

YARN

Yarn seems like a simple enough embellishment, that is, until you start to explore specialty yarns. The variety of color and textures that can be found in the yarn aisle of your local craft store is enough to convince you to definitely start adding some to your layouts.

RAFFIA

Raffia is most often found in its natural color, which closely resembles wheat or hay. You can also find it in several shades of dyed colors. Simply tie raffia through the hole in the top of a tag or wrap it around a journaling box to add some natural-looking dimension to your page.

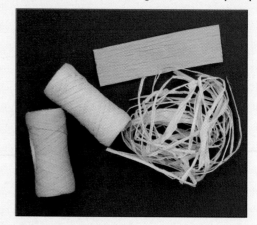

This layout shows an example of what you can do with fibers. The raffia on this page could easily be replaced with yarn, ribbon, or floss on similar pages with different themes and color schemes. To add the raffia around the page, holes are punched first and then raffia is simply threaded through each hole.

Stitching with Floss

Hand-stitching is for more than sewing a button on your shirt. Simple stitching can make a very effective page embellishment. The best part is that by following these steps, it is quick and easy to do.

Make a Flower

1. Select a die-cut to use as a basic pattern. Trace around the pattern lightly with a pencil on your background cardstock. If needed, add some lines on the inside of the design for interest.

2. Use a push-pin to poke small holes evenly along the pencil lines. Carefully erase the pencil lines before stitching.

3. Thread your needle with embroidery floss and stitch along the dotted lines all the way around the design.

4. Repeat these steps for additional designs on your scrapbook page.

The stitched flowers on this page accent the stitching on the dress of the little girl and her doll. By keeping the shapes simple, the page designer is able to stitch this page in just a few minutes.

Printing on Textures

Dimensional items such as cork, ribbon, and fabric can also be exciting title or journaling enhancements. Printing on these items takes a few special considerations.

Printing on Sheet Cork

1. Start by printing on regular office paper the words and phrases that you wish to print on textured material.

2. Use a repositionable adhesive to adhere the fabric, very thin sheet cork, or ribbon over the printed words. Use small chunks of fabric or cork, allowing the margins of the paper to remain free to guide the paper through the printer.

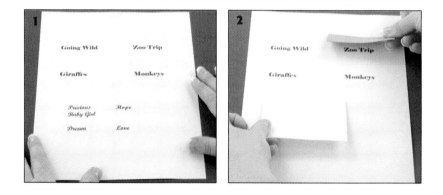

3. All printers are different. Be careful not to damage your printer by printing on materials that are too thick for it.

4. Place the sheet back in the printer and print again; this time the printing appears on top of the textured material.

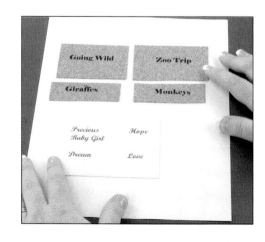

This layout uses printed sheet cork. The thin cork is only slightly thicker than cardstock. Be careful running thick items through your printer to prevent jamming and damage. If you are concerned, you could achieve a similar look by rubber stamping on the cork instead.

Household Embellishments

Scrapbooking can be an expensive hobby, but not all page decorations need to be costly. Look at items that you may have around the house, and be inspired to create your next page.

SEWING NOTIONS

Start looking for household embellishments by raiding the sewing box. Zippers, buttons, and rickrack are all perfect page decorations.

OFFICE SUPPLIES

Next stop on your household embellishment hunt is the office desk. Spiral paper clips, document clips, and even staples make great-looking fasteners on scrapbook pages.

FOUND ITEMS

Now look everywhere else and you will find things such as bottle caps, floral pebbles, sea glass, and mini-clothespins. Many of these items are manufactured in small sizes and various colors just for scrapbooking.

This scrapbook page layout uses sewing notions (a zipper and rickrack) and office supplies (staples and paper clips) as embellishments. The effect is a layout that has plenty of dimension, with very little impact on the scrapbooking budget.

Working with Wire

When you are ready to try out some more advanced scrapbooking techniques, you will definitely want to try working with wire. You only need a few tools and a little bit of instruction to get started making beautiful scrapbook pages with wire.

Craft Wire Basics

Wire comes in a variety of types, colors, and gauges. In order to select the right wire for your scrapbook project, you need to understand your choices.

CRAFT WIRE

Quality craft wire for use in scrapbooks is permanent colored copper wire. This means that the wire itself is copper that has gone through the process of being colored and sealed. This wire is flexible, strong, and will not deteriorate in your albums. When you cut it, especially the heavier gauges, you can see the copper core.

COLORS

Permanent colored copper wire comes in nearly every imaginable color. You can find colors to match any scrapbook page you design. Copper, silver, and black wire can be used on a variety of pages.

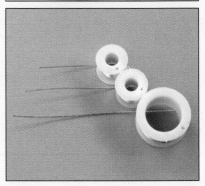

THICKNESS

Wire thickness is measured in "gauges." The higher the number, the thinner the wire; conversely, the lower the number, the thicker the wire. In general, thicker wire such as 20 or 22 gauge is perfect for fashioning words out of wire. Very thin wire, such as 26 gauge, is good for wrapping around cardstock or brads, while 24-gauge wire is a good choice for general wire work such as making shapes and designs.

To get started working with wire, you need three basic tools. Each can be found at your local craft store or online.

WIRE CUTTERS

The first tool you need for wire working is a pair of wire cutters. Just as the name suggests, wire cutters are used to cut wire. Using scissors to cut wire can damage the blades.

NYLON JAW PLIERS

Another essential tool for wire working is a pair of nylon jaw pliers. These pliers have a nylon (a form of plastic) jaw, which allows you to grab and hold the wire without damaging its colored surface. They are also used for straightening wire.

ROUND NOSE PLIERS

The only other tool you need to get started working with wire is a pair of round nose pliers. Unlike their cousin, the needle nose pliers, round nose pliers have tips that are completely round. They are designed for making loops in the wire.

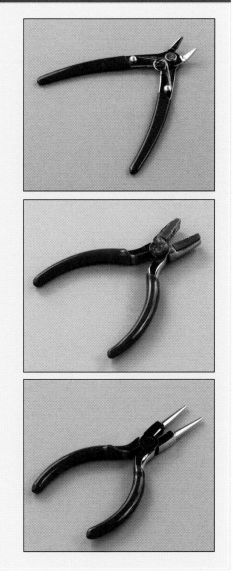

Straightening Wire

Your wire designs will only look as perfect as the wire is when you begin. To get the wire perfectly smooth, you need to straighten it.

Make It Smooth

1. Unroll from the wire spool the amount of wire you intend to work with for the first part of your project. For many wire words and other embellishments, start with a piece that is as long as the distance from your pinched fingers down to your elbow.

2. Do not cut the wire off of the spool but rather hook it back in the notch.

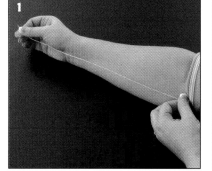
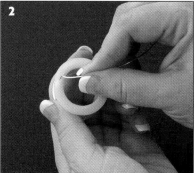

3. Firmly grasp the wire near the spool with the nylon jaw pliers.

4. Pull the wire through the jaws of the tool all the way down its length. Repeat two times until the wire is smooth and straight.

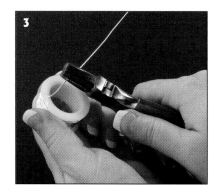
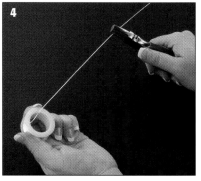

The most basic shape in wire working is the loop. These simple steps start you on your way to making more intricate designs.

Round It Out

1. Start with a piece of straightened wire. The wire shown here is 20 gauge. Grasp the very end of the wire firmly between the tips of the round nose pliers. The end of the wire should be hidden inside the tips of the tool.

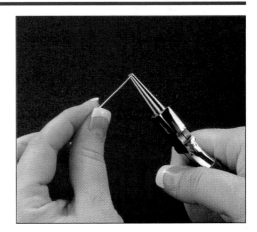

2. Use your thumb to firmly press the wire tightly around one of the two tips of the tool.

3. Release the wire and remove it from the tip of the round nose pliers and you should have a perfect little loop on the end. If needed, slip the tip back into the loop and turn the wire slightly more to close up the loop.

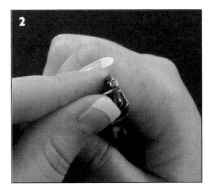

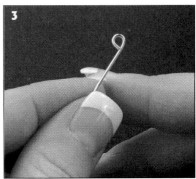

Tight Spirals

Once you have a loop, the next basic design is a spiral. Tight spirals can themselves be used as page embellishments. Picture them as wire polka dots.

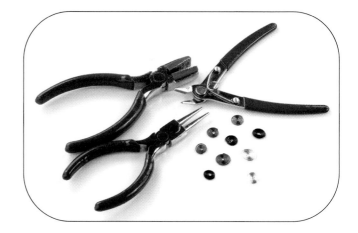

Curl It Up

1. Begin with a straightened piece of 24-gauge or thicker wire. Make a loop on the end of the wire.

2. Use nylon jaw pliers to grasp the side of the loop and begin turning it so that it appears to roll down the length of the wire.

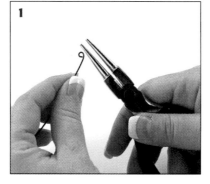

3. As you continue to turn the growing spiral, be sure to pull it tightly back toward the length of wire, maintaining an even spiral.

4. When the spiral is the desired size, use wire cutters to snip it off from the length of wire. Tight spirals can be attached to your layout with liquid adhesive, photo tape, or GlueDots™.

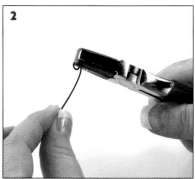

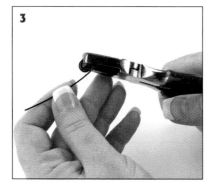

Loose Spirals

Loose spirals are a basic design in wire writing and other wire embellishments. With a little practice, you can make nice even spirals every time.

Loose Curls

1. Begin with a straightened piece of 24-gauge or thicker wire. Make a loop on the end of the wire.

2. Use nylon jaw pliers to grasp the side of the loop and begin turning it so that it appears to roll down the length of the wire. As you turn it, be sure to allow a space between each turn of the spiral.

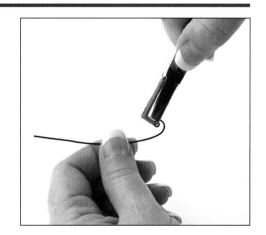

3. As you continue to turn the growing spiral, try to keep the spacing equal (a). Continue turning until the spiral is the size you wish. Use wire cutters to snip off the spiral from the length of wire (b).

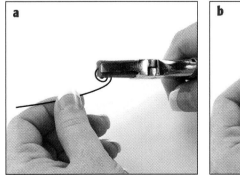

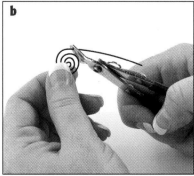

Simple Wire Embellishments

By combining the skills you now have in making loops and spirals, you can create beautiful scrapbook page decorations such as these simple embellished leaves.

Embellished Leaves

1. Use a push-pin to poke a hole in the top and bottom of a die-cut leaf.

2. Thread a 4" long piece of straightened 24-gauge copper wire through the holes, coming up from the back through the bottom hole and going in from the top through the top hole.

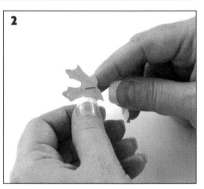

3. Fold a ½" long piece of wire through to the back behind the top hole pinching it tight to hold it in place.

4. Finish the leaf by creating a loop and loose spiral on the end of the wire. Adhere the wire to your scrapbook page with your favorite adhesive.

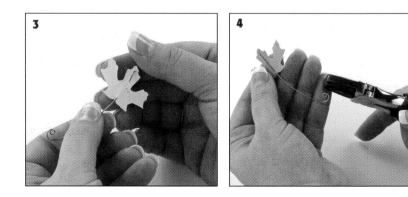

This completed layout uses the copper wire embellished leaves as accents in several places on the page to complement the copper wire title "discover nature."

Wire Words

Making words from wire is easier than you might think. Use these guidelines and with a little practice, you will be making perfect letters in no time.

Your First Wire Word: "Love"

1. The easiest way to begin any wire word is by sketching out the word on a piece of scrap paper. Write it in cursive, using a flowing font that you could imagine being designed from wire. Select a color of 20-gauge wire to work with; the sample shown uses silver.

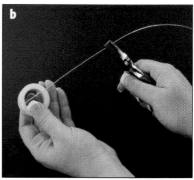

2. Estimate how much wire you need to create the word. In this case, for a simple four-letter word, wire from your fingertips to your elbow should be plenty (a). Straighten this piece of wire and cut it off the spool (b).

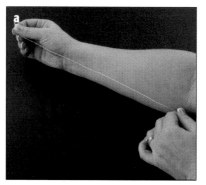

③ Using your sketch as a guide, begin with the first letter. Wire words look finished when you start and end with a loop and spiral. The spiral can be simple and small or large and fancy. For this word, create a loop on the end of the wire and then add a couple of turns for a simple loose spiral.

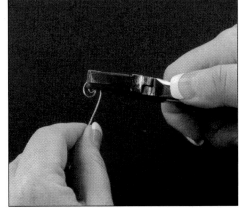

④ After the spiral, decide the height of the first letter in your word. About three fingers high works for the "L." At the bottom of the letter bend the wire around to form a loop and send it in the direction of the rest of the word.

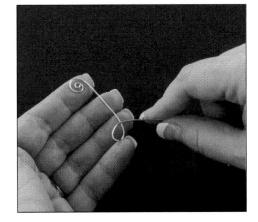

⑤ To create the "o," the easiest thing to do is loosely wrap the wire around your pinky. The wire from the top of the "o" goes out to the "v."

CONTINUED ON NEXT PAGE

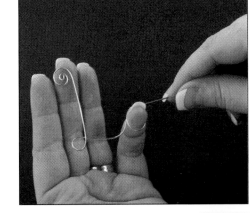

6 The "v" is an easy bend down (a) and then up (b), sending the wire in the direction of the "e."

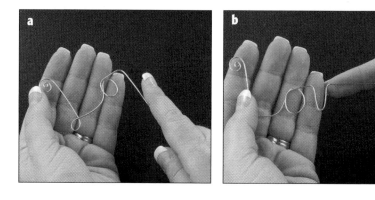

7 The "e" is a simple loop around.

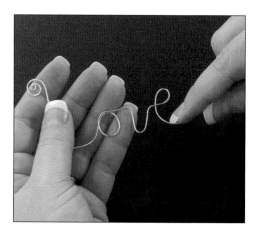

8 To finish the word, you will need to trim off the excess wire, leaving 1" to finish the word.

9 Once you cut off the extra, make a loop on the end of the wire and turn it in toward the "e" to complete the final loose spiral.

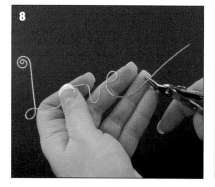

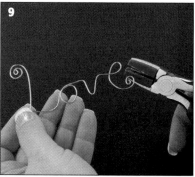

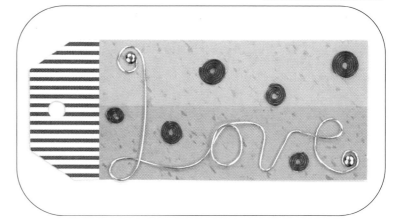

Once you master creating designs and words with wire, the next obvious question is, "How do I attach them to my scrapbook pages?" These three techniques make attaching wire to your layouts simple.

Adhere Wire to Pages

ADHESIVE DOT

1 Any wire embellishments that have significant surface area, such as tight spirals, can be attached to the page with an **adhesive dot.** Simply press the dot to the layout where you wish to adhere the spiral.

2 Press the spiral on to the adhesive. Continue adding spirals to decorate the layout.

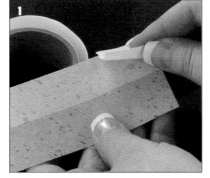

MATCHING MINI-BRAD

Wire designs that have a loop included in them, such as a wire word, can be quickly attached by using a matching mini-brad. Use a pin to poke a hole through the loop into the cardstock below. Press the brad through the hole and open the prongs on the back to finish.

CONTINUED ON NEXT PAGE

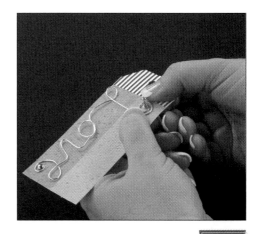

WIRE STAPLES

1 Create wire staples to attach any wire embellishment to your page without having to use any additional tools or adhesives. To begin, cut a 1" length of the same color wire you have been using to make the word or design.

2 Fold this piece of wire in half, creating something that resembles a bobby pin.

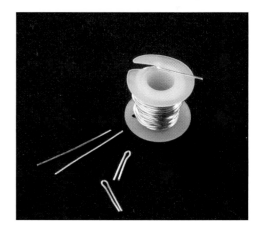

3 Place the wire embellishment on the background cardstock and use a pin to poke a hole slightly inside and one outside the wire.

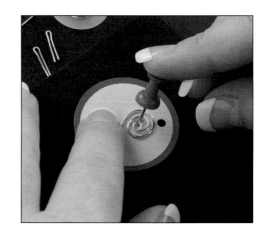

4 Insert the bent wire through these two holes to the back of the paper, capturing the wire design and holding it to the page.

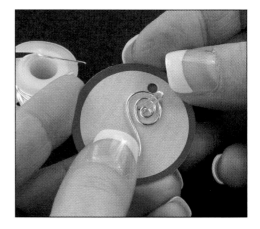

⑤ Open the two prongs of the folded wire as if it were a brad.

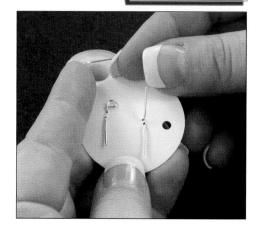

⑥ To keep the wire from slipping out of the holes, use your round nose pliers to make a loop on each end of the wire, locking it in place on the back of the page. This leaves a neat and clean backing and a solidly attached embellishment.

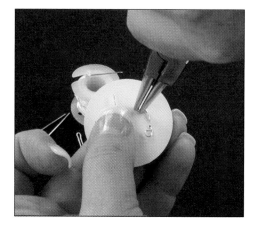

FAQ

How many wire staples do I need to attach my words to my layouts?

You only need to use two or three staples per word to firmly attach your wire words to your pages. They hold very securely, making additional attachments unnecessary.

Beaded Dragonfly

From simple embellishments to intricate-looking designs, the same basic techniques are all you need. This gorgeous dragonfly is broken down for you in easy-to-follow steps.

1. Start with an 18" piece of 24-gauge sea-foam green wire. Leave a 3" tail on one end and wrap the rest of the wire around your first two fingers in figure-eight style until you have circled each finger twice.

2. Wrap the longest of the two tails around the center of the figure eight tightly two times to tie it off. End the wrapping with the two tails going in opposite directions.

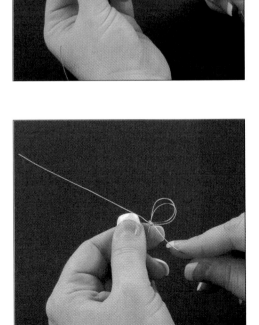

③ Add one (size 6) seed bead to the longest tail to form the dragonfly's head (a), then fold the tail down to match up with the opposite tail. Trim so that the wires are equal length (b).

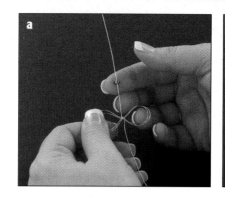
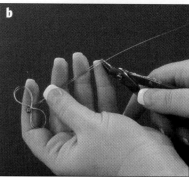

④ Add nine more (size 6) seed beads over both of the two wires (a). Fold the ends of the tails out to keep the beads from sliding off of the wire (b).

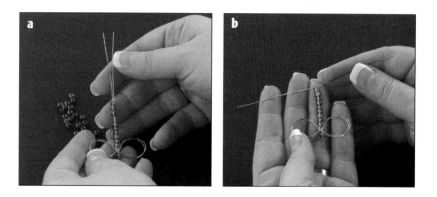

⑤ If needed, trim the wire so that the two tails are each 1" long (a). Loop and spiral the ends back toward the dragonfly (b).

CONTINUED ON NEXT PAGE

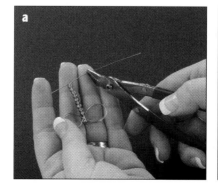
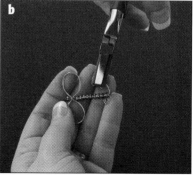

6. Carefully spread the wings open (a) and gently pull them to create a long, oval-shaped wing (b).

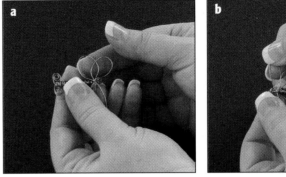
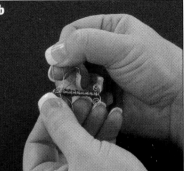

7. Use a toothpick to apply liquid craft glue to the back of each wing.

8. Apply a small piece of iridescent fabric to the glued surfaces and let dry completely.

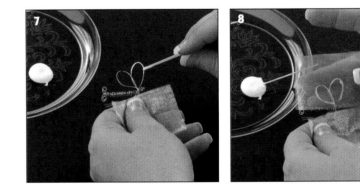

9. When dry, trim around the outside of the wire wings, leaving the fabric glued in the center. Attach dragonflies to your layout by gluing the beaded bodies with adhesive dots or liquid glue.

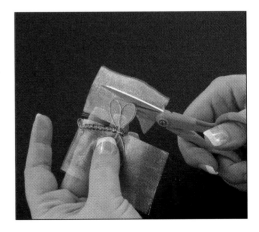

This layout uses three beaded dragonflies in a dimensional page border. The dragonfly embellishments enhance the garden theme of the page.

Beaded flowers make wonderful spring or wedding scrapbook pages. These simple steps show you how to make them in just minutes.

Flower Steps

1. Start with an 18" piece of 24-gauge wire in any shade. Add five purple (size 6) seed beads to the end of the wire.

2. Bring the wire around to make a loop of beads, and wrap and trim to tie it off. This is the center of your flower.

3. Each of the petals will wrap around one of the beads in the center. To begin, add smaller seed beads or a variety of tiny seed and bugle beads to the wire until you fill approximately 1¾" of wire with beads.

④ Bring the wire around and through the closest bead on the center ring. Pull it tight until the first petal forms.

⑤ Before you begin beading the next petal, feed the wire through the next bead in the center.

⑥ Once again bead 1¾" of wire and repeat the last two steps for each petal.

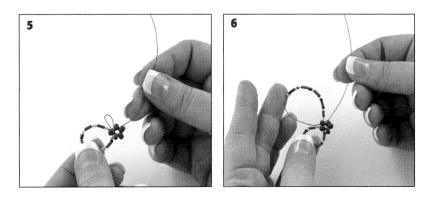

⑦ After all of the petals are formed, wrap the remaining wire tightly around the wire that forms the center loop two times to tie it off (a). Use wire cutters to snip off any remaining wire, and your flower is complete (b).

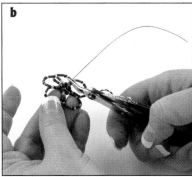

12

Get Organized

Once you start gathering supplies, you will realize that the only way to get any scrapbooking done is to be organized. Some tough organizational questions for scrapbookers include how do I store all of this oversized paper? How do I sort all of these tiny embellishments? Simple steps and homemade solutions help you get organized and ready to create beautiful scrapbook pages.

Bring-It-Along Storage

Most scrapbookers need two types of storage: bring-it-along storage and stay-at-home storage. The types of bags and totes shown here can help you organize all of the materials that you need to take with you when you go to a scrapbooking party with friends.

Bag Your Stuff

BACKPACK

Carry bags are storage for scrapbook basics. Be conservative with what you load into them to keep the weight manageable. The bag shown here is actually a backpack. You can fill it with all of your basics plus several page kits and have enough material to scrapbook for hours without being weighed down with extras.

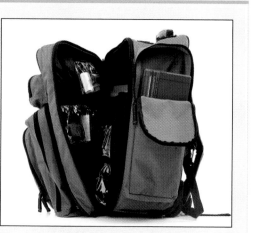

BINDER STORAGE

Binder storage is ideal for stickers, rub-ons, and other embellishments. Clear plastic divider sheets enable you to organize your supplies.

LARGE CARRY BAG

Larger carry bags are designed to hold an album, 12" × 12" paper, and all the supplies needed to scrapbook. This bag is just right for someone getting started in scrapbooking, or for an advanced scrapbooker who needs to add storage to her wheeled tote.

SMALL WHEELED BAGS

Wheeled bags can handle the weight of your paper and scrapbooking supplies. Need to fly somewhere and want to bring your scrapbooking supplies along for when you get there? Handy carry-on size wheeled bags are just the answer. This case has a convenient built-in seat.

FULL-SIZED WHEELED BAG

Sometimes you just need to bring along a lot of supplies. Maybe you will be away from home for some time, or perhaps you don't know what you want to work on in your scrapbooks. Full-sized wheeled storage bags like this one can hold just about everything. If you need even more space, simply combine one of these large wheeled bags with one or more of the smaller bags previously described.

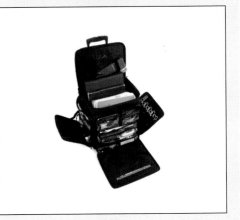

Paper Storage

The number-one dilemma in organizing scrapbooking supplies is $12" \times 12"$ paper storage. Choose the organizational system that works best for your scrapbook area.

Paper Organization Choices

STACKING TRAYS

Clear stacking trays enable you to see all of your paper at one time. Add more trays as your paper stash grows.

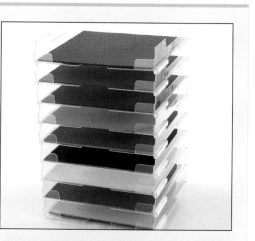

ROLLING TOWER

These stacking trays become moveable when you put them on a rolling base. You can slide the rolling tower under a table or desktop when not in use.

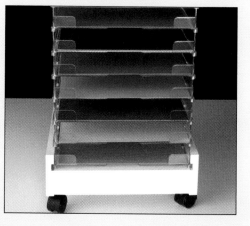

HANGING FILE FOLDERS

Horizontal paper storage such as stacking trays takes up a significant amount of space in your scrapbook room. If you need storage on a more compact scale, consider vertical storage such as 12" × 12" hanging file folders.

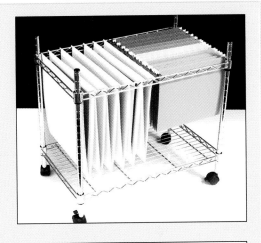

STORAGE BOXES

Paper storage boxes can each hold up to 250 sheets of paper, making these the most efficient use of storage space for scrapbookers.

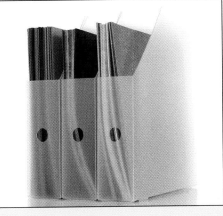

ENVELOPES

Store scraps of paper based on color or theme in clear office supply envelopes. Be sure to get envelopes that tie or snap shut to keep smaller pieces inside. You can then store the envelopes in any of the storage systems previously discussed.

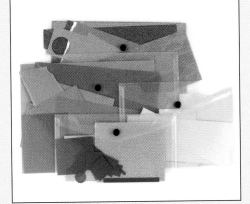

Make Your Own Storage Cubes

Storage cubes are most often used in college dorm rooms, but with a few adjustments they can become perfect storage for scrapbook paper. The best part about these cube sets is that they are both inexpensive and easy to assemble.

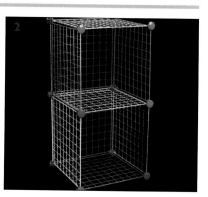

Create Cubes

1. Purchase a cube storage kit at a discount store. Also, buy a package of wire ties ("zip-ties").

2. Follow package instructions to put together half of the available number of cubes in the kit.

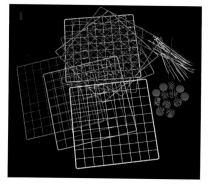

3. Use the leftover panels to divide each assembled cube into smaller sections. Use the plastic wire ties to secure the panels in place, dividing each cube to create three or four storage spaces.

4. Fill with paper, stickers, idea books, etc.

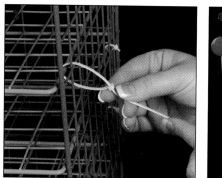
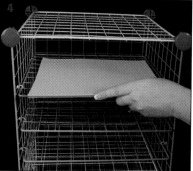

Storage cubes work well for paper, but a pegboard wall can organize many of your other scrapbook supplies. Embellishments, fiber cards, and tools can all find a place on this do-it-yourself project.

Build the Wall

1. Frame out the back of two pieces of 2' × 4' pegboard with 1" × 2" lumber by screwing through the pegboard into the lumber, giving stability to both boards.

2. Attach a pair of hinges to the 1" × 2" pieces, creating a hinged, free-standing pegboard wall.

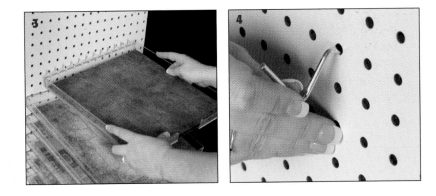

3. Add paper trays for 12" × 12" paper storage.

4. Add hooks and other accessories found at home improvement centers to hang additional tools and supplies.

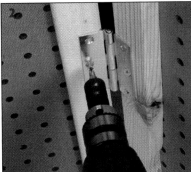

Embellishment Storage

The popularity of using metal attach-ments, such as eyelets, brads, hinges, and nailheads, in scrapbooking has given rise to the need to store and organize all of these tiny bits. You can purchase organizational solutions for small embellishments, or with a little creativity you can make them yourself.

Store the Small Stuff

STORAGE CONTAINERS

Manufacturers have come to the rescue when it comes to storing embellishments. These small boxes can each be labeled and then placed in an embellishment storage box (a). This system keeps every-thing in its place and right at your fingertips when you are working (b).

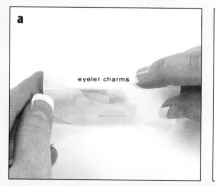

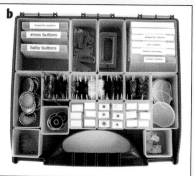

ROUND PLASTIC BOXES

Clear, round, plastic boxes also hold a large amount of small embellishments. Each one can be filled and slipped into a storage device designed for them.

SPICE JARS

Make your own embellishment storage out of a spice rack. This one turns and holds 16 storage jars. Each jar can be labeled with a label maker or the labels from the original embellishment packaging can be carefully peeled off and attached to the jars.

DO-IT-YOURSELF STORAGE

Additional do-it-yourself storage can be made out of salvaged materials such as mint boxes and topping shakers (a). Keep an eye out for boxes in your kitchen that when empty could be used as embellishment storage instead of being thrown away.

Lastly, there is no need to re-invent the wheel. When it comes to storing small items, storage has been available for a long time at your local home improvement center. Garage or workroom storage boxes and drawers work perfectly for scrapbook embellishment storage (b).

Make Your Fiber Organizer Cards

Storing yarns, fibers, and ribbon can be a challenge. These page decorations have a tendency to pile up and get tangled. Easy-to-make yarn cards can be stored in a photo box or hung on pegs on a pegboard wall.

Make the Card

1. Cut chipboard to size. The card shown here measures 4" × 8". This enables you to get four cards from one piece of 12" ×12 " chipboard.

2. Use a ruler to measure and mark 1" marks down each side of the card.

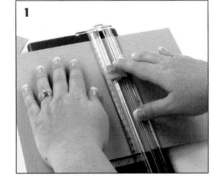
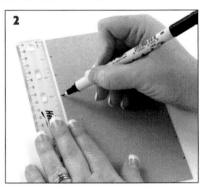

3. Use an office hole punch to punch notches along the sides at each mark. Snap off the guide that fills with the punched circles of paper, so that when you turn the punch upside down you will be able to see exactly where you are punching. Insert the card only halfway into the punch so that the hole you punch will be a semi-circle.

4. Measure to find the center and punch a hanging hole ½" from the top center of the card. This can be used to hang the finished card from a pegboard organizing wall.

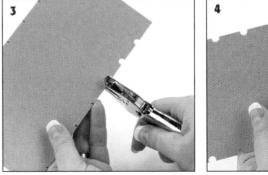

⑤ Cut a small slit (approximately ¼"
long) between each of the notches
down one side of the card.

⑥ Add yarns by wrapping them around
the card. Finish wrapping each color
by slipping the end of the yarn into the
slit to hold it in place.

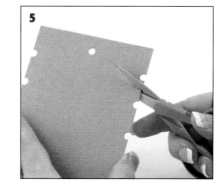

⑦ To add ribbon to the card (a), double
punch the side notches creating a
bigger slot so that the ribbon can
lie flat (b).

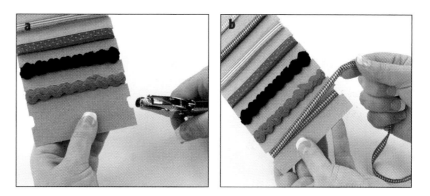

Mini and Theme Scrapbooks

Scrapbooks make wonderful gifts. Full-size scrapbooks, however, can take months to complete. Mini and theme scrapbooks, on the other hand, can be completed in a weekend and make the perfect gift for any occasion. Try one of these fun and rewarding projects this weekend and you will see just how easy it can be to complete a tiny scrapbook.

Basic Mini-Books

Scrapbooks can come in all shapes and sizes. This simple mini-book is a great, stand-alone gift or small theme album. You can also use it on a scrapbook page to give yourself more room for extra photos and journaling. The mini-book shown here is used as a "Baby's First Year" mini-album, perfect for a proud grandma to carry in her purse.

Make the Mini-Book

1. Trim a piece of chipboard (the cardboard on the back of a pad of paper) into two pieces. Each piece should measure 6" × 4½".

2. Choose a piece of printed paper for the cover of the book. Cut this piece to 7" × 10½".

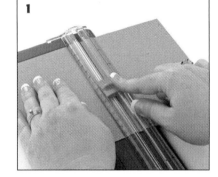

3. Adhere the chipboard pieces to the back of the cover paper, leaving a half-inch between them and making sure that equal amounts of the paper are showing on all sides.

4. Fold each corner in toward the center of the chipboard as shown and glue in place.

⑤ Fold the remaining edges of the paper around the chipboard and use photo tape to adhere them firmly into place.

⑥ Cut two pieces of ribbon that are each 9" long. Adhere each piece to the back of the chipboard as shown, using photo tape.

⑦ Make the inside pages by cutting at least three or as many as seven pieces of cardstock to 8½" × 5½".

⑧ Fold each piece exactly in half and press with a bone folder to get a nice, sharp crease.

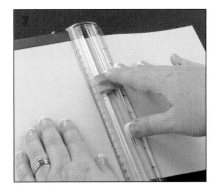

⑨ Adhere each folded piece back to back with another piece as shown. Continue until all pieces have been adhered together. They will look like the pages of a book.

⑩ Adhere the pages to the inside of the completed cover.

CONTINUED ON NEXT PAGE

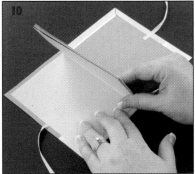

Basic Mini-Book: Baby's First Year

After you complete the book, you can pick a theme and add photos, journaling, and simple embellishments. Because the theme for this book is "Baby's First Year," the book has dated tabs that mark the months.

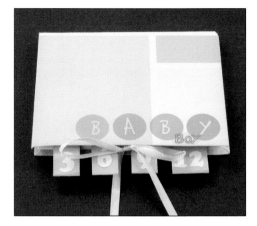

① To add photos to the book, simply trim a 4" × 6" photo slightly to fill the page. Smaller photos such as 3" ×5" or wallet-size portraits can be matted to fill the page.

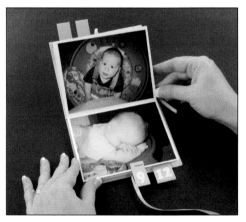

② To add tabs to the book, cut strips of paper or cardstock that are 3½"× ½". Fold each strip in half.

③ Add a sticker or rub-on number to the tab and staple it to the edge of the album page

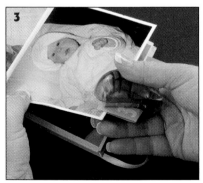

To use a mini-book on a scrapbook page, all you need to do is adhere it with some photo tape to your page. You may want to add some chipboard to the back of the scrapbook page to give it added stability to hold the weight of the book. On this layout, ultrasound photos of the baby are housed in a mini-book.

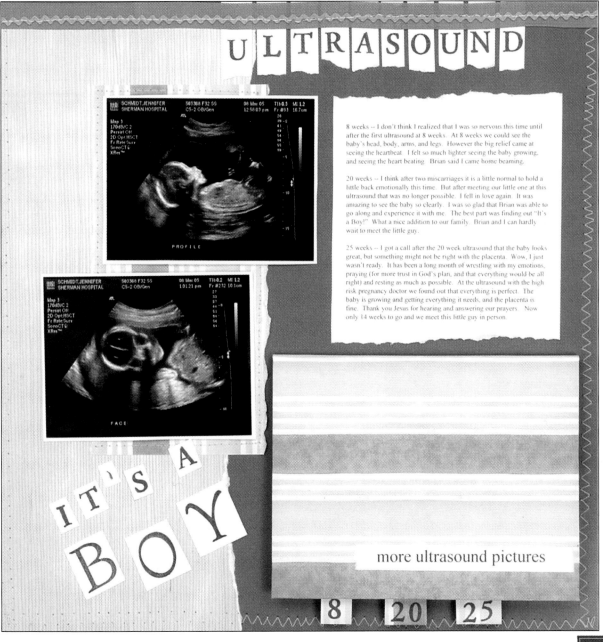

Tag Albums

Tags can be used for photo mats, journaling boxes, and even shaker embellishments. By attaching tags together you can create a tag mini book. This small scrapbook can then be filled with photos and journaling to match any theme.

Make the Tag Album

1. Cut 4" × 12" strips of cardstock from a 12" square sheet. Each strip makes two book pages.

2. Fold each strip in half and crease firmly.

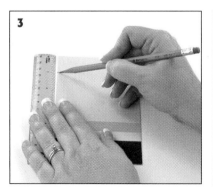
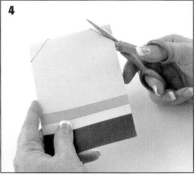

3. Use a ruler and a pencil to measure and mark the sides and top of the folded edge of each strip. Mark 1" down the side and 1" in toward the center on the folded edge.

4. Connect these marks to draw a line at an angle across the top of the folded strip. Cut on these lines to create your tag shapes.

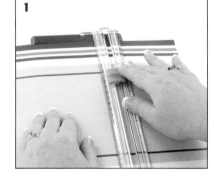
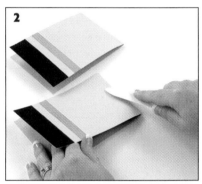

5. Fold each tag over a ruler ¾" from the top folded edge to crease the pages of the book so they will turn freely.

6. Once creased, apply adhesive to the inside of the folded tag above the crease line to adhere the top of the tag closed.

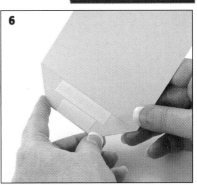

7. Once all tags have been creased and glued, apply adhesive above the crease line on the front of a tag and adhere it to the back of another tag.

8. Continue until all tags are attached together, forming the book.

9. Measure and mark the center, ½" from the top of the front tag of the book.

10. Use a push pin to make a hole that goes through all the layers of tags. Add a decorative brad through this hole to complete the book.

CONTINUED ON NEXT PAGE

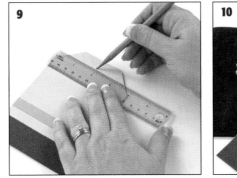

Tag Album: Favorite Photos

Your creativity is the only limitation when it comes to embellishing your tag book. The tag mini-book shown here becomes a "Sisters and Friends" mini-scrapbook that showcases favorite photos of the two girls together over the years. It is decorated with pre-printed stickers and ribbon.

EMBELLISHING THE ALBUM

1 The ribbon at the top of the album is held in place by the mini-brad. Start with a 4" long piece of ribbon that you carefully fold in half at an angle, keeping the top side facing up.

2 Hold the ribbon in place as you poke a hole through it with the push pin.

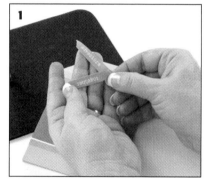

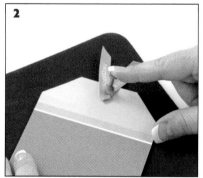

3 Add the brad through the hole, securing the ribbon to the book.

4 Complete the cover embellishment by adding more ribbon and some definition stickers. A title is printed on vellum and also attached with mini-brads.

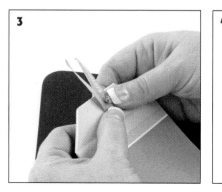

Tag Album: School Days

The tag mini-book shown here can be used to hold precious school days photos. A "First Day of School" theme album could contain photos of "firsts" over the years.

TEARING THE PAGES

1 Assemble the book using a different color of cardstock for each 4" wide strip.

2 Starting from the last page, carefully tear each tag slightly shorter than the next. This allows the color of each page to show to the front.

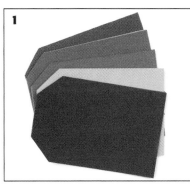

3 Ink or chalk the edges of each page.

4 Add ribbon and a charm to the front of the album to complete the embellishment.

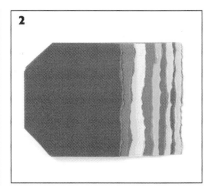

Envelope Mini-Books

Envelopes come in a variety of sizes, shapes, and colors. By using these often-overlooked items to create a scrapbook, your pages automatically have pockets to contain journaling tags or precious memorabilia. The book shown here would be perfect for pictures to help you remember a weekend at the beach.

Make the Envelope Mini-Book

1. Begin with an odd number of envelopes that are all the same size and shape.

2. Adhere the flap of one envelope to the bottom edge of the back of the next envelope.

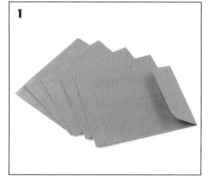
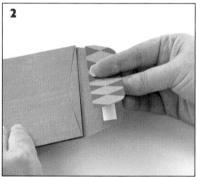

3. Continue until all envelopes are attached in a long chain. Fan-fold the envelopes back and forth so that they close in a neat stack.

4. If the flap on the final envelope contains adhesive, cover it with a coordinating piece of paper to prevent humidity from causing it to stick to the album in the future.

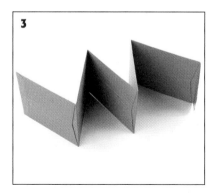
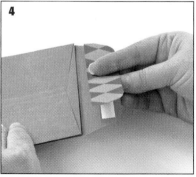

5 Add paper and stickers to embellish the cover of the book.

6 Rub-ons, stickers, or transparencies can be used to add a title and subtitles to the album.

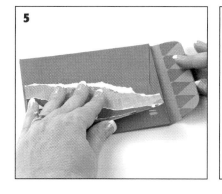

7 Trim photos slightly so that they fit on each page of the album.

8 Add journaling on tags cut to fit inside each pocket of the book.

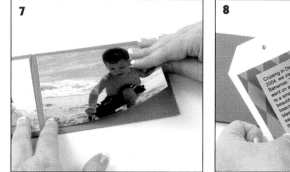

9 Tie a ribbon or floss around the whole book as a closure.

CONTINUED ON NEXT PAGE

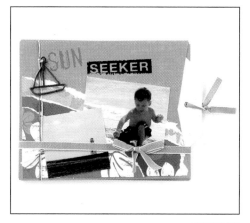

Envelope Mini-Book: Travel

The book shown here is a travel journal of a family's trip to Russia to adopt a child. The album is embellished to fit an Old-World travel theme.

EMBELLISHING THE COVER

1. The envelope album itself is made of rust-colored envelopes. To begin embellishing the cover, add a pre-made closure to the final flap.

2. Cut and tear on an angle map-printed paper and weathered cardstock to size to fit across the cover of the book.

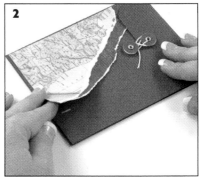

3. Ink the surfaces with brown ink and the edges with black ink.

4. Add rub-on travel words and the letters for the title.

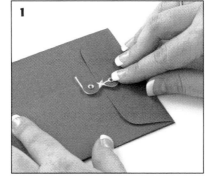

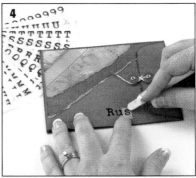

⑤ To fill the album, start by inking the surface of each page with brown ink, just as you did on the cover. Also, ink all the edges with black.

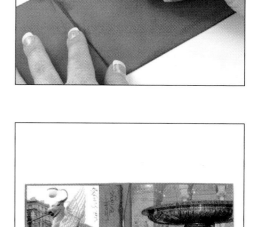

⑥ Trim the photos and adhere them to each page. Handwritten, rub-on, or sticker titles may be added to each page.

⑦ Ink tags for the pockets and use these to hold memorabilia, such as tickets, receipts, and small maps.

Accordion Scrapbooks

These exciting mini-scrapbooks pop open to display photos, journaling, and small embellishments. The intricate design looks much more difficult to create than it really is.

Make an Accordion Album

1. Cut two 4½" × 4½" pieces of chipboard, two 5½" × 5½" pieces of paper for the cover of the book, three 8" square pieces of cardstock, and a 16" piece of ribbon.

2. Cover the chipboard pieces with the two paper pieces intended for the cover by adhering the chipboard to the back center of the paper, trimming the corners, and folding over and gluing the edges.

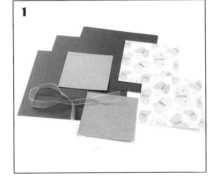

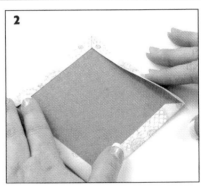

3. Adhere a piece of ribbon at least 16" long across the back of one of the cover pieces.

4. Score three lines on each of the 8" squares, as shown here. Paper with different shades front and back are shown here to make it easier to see the construction of the album.

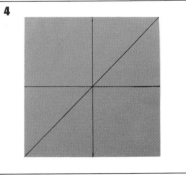

⑤ Fold on each of the three scored lines and open.

⑥ Fold each square into a smaller square by creating "mountain folds" along the diagonal score line. Bring these folds together toward the center of the square.

⑦ Finish the fold by pressing the two smaller squares together.

⑧ Fold all three squares in this manner and you will have three folded pieces that look like this.

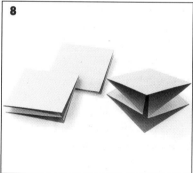

⑨ Turn the center piece over so that you can overlap the small squares on each piece. Adhere these squares together.

⑩ Use photo tape to secure the folded pages to the inside of the book covers, being sure to center them on the back of each cover. The ribbon is used to secure the book closed.

CONTINUED ON NEXT PAGE

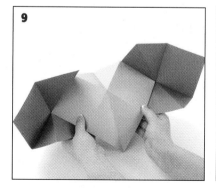
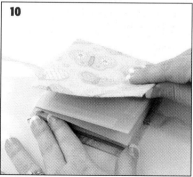

Accordion Scrapbook: Template

Both square and triangular photos can be added to an accordion book. The book shown here has an "Extreme Sports" theme and is filled with photos of both shapes that complement this theme. Cutting triangular photos is easier if you first create a template.

MAKING A TEMPLATE

1. Cut a piece of semi-transparent plastic, such as a plastic folder from an office supply store, into a 3¾" square.

2. Cut the square in half on the diagonal to create two triangle templates the perfect size for this album.

3. Lay the template over a photo and trace with a photo marking pencil or pen.

4. Cut on the traced lines.

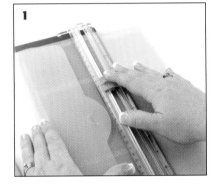

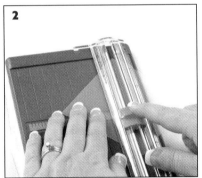

Make a Keychain Accordion Book

Accordion albums can be made in a variety of sizes. By reducing the dimensions of the larger book, you can make an adorable mini-album to add to your keychain or carry in your purse. The album shown here is a mini-scrapbook with a Christmas theme.

ADDING A KEYCHAIN

1 To add a keychain to a mini-accordion album, use a hole punch to make a hole in one corner of the album.

2 Set an eyelet in this hole.

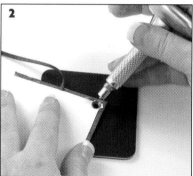

3 Add a key ring chain through the hole.

4 Finish the album by adding small pictures and journaling.

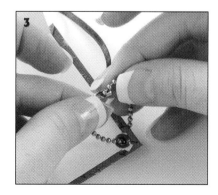

Paper Bag Albums

Once you start thinking about things that could be turned into scrapbooks, you never know what you might come up with. How about lunch bags? Yes, paper lunch bags can become an adorable mini-scrapbook. Since paper bags are not necessarily acid-free, be sure to use copies of your photos for this project.

Make the Album

1. Gather six paper lunch bags. Stack the bags right-side up with the ends of every other bag going in opposite directions.

2. Ink the edges of all six bags. This step is much easier to complete before you finish assembling the book.

3. Fold the bags in half to crease the center line. Use a sewing machine to sew down the center of the bags.

4. Cut a strip of printed paper to 5¼" × 4". Adhere this strip of paper to the back of the stack of pages. Center the strip over the sewn line.

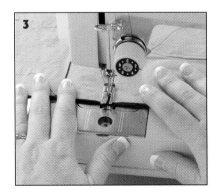

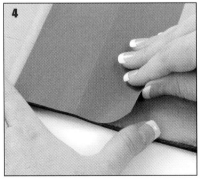

⑤ Punch holes for eyelets ½" apart down one side of the center strip.

⑥ Set eyelets in each of these holes.

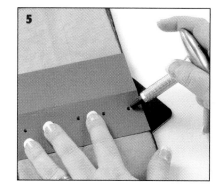
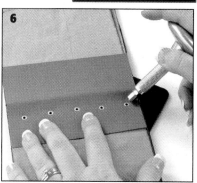

⑦ Fold the book closed. Use a pen to mark through the eyelets to the pages beneath to indicate where you need to place the eyelets for the other side.

⑧ Open the book, punch holes at the pen marks, and set the eyelets in the holes.

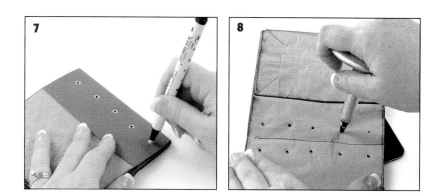

⑨ Close the book. Tie lengths of ribbon through the holes to attach the front to the back of the book and hold everything in place.

CONTINUED ON NEXT PAGE

Anniversary Book

Paper bag books can be made for any theme. This gorgeous anniversary-theme scrapbook details the "10 Things I Love About You After 10 Years." The pages are decorated with a cohesive color scheme of black, white, and red.

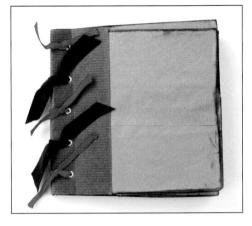

A PEEK INSIDE

Each pair of pages in this album is decorated with a number that reflects the "10 Things" plus one or more photos that follow the theme.

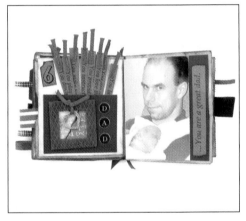

Each opening in the paper bags has tags slipped into it that allow extra room for journaling.

Friends Book

Paper bags do not have to be inked and chalked. They can, instead, have clean lines and bright colors. This "Friends" album shows how paper bag scrapbooks can be decorated with pink and purple, to highlight photos of little girls.

A PEEK INSIDE

Extra-large paint strips from the paint department of a local home center are inserted into the bag openings as journaling tags. A small piece of ribbon attached to the tag makes each tag easier to remove from the book. The cover is embellished with silk flowers and mini-brads.

The inside of the book details what makes sisters such good friends. The pages are filled with photos of the girls and great quotes about the special relationship shared by sisters.

Container Books

Little albums can be made more durable by encasing them in containers. Mint tins, CD cases, or die boxes all can be turned into container scrapbooks. Dies used with Sizzix™ die cutting machines come in clear plastic boxes that are perfect cases for a container book.

Create a Die Box Album

1. Start with a plastic case. Here, a Sizzix™ die case for larger dies is used; it is approximately 5" × 5½" in size. Spray-paint the outside of the case and let it dry completely.

2. Decorate the painted case with rubber stamping, rub-ons, stickers, ribbon, and charms.

3. Cut three strips of cardstock 5" × 12".

4. Use photo tape to attach the end of each strip to the next one to create one strip of cardstock almost 36" long.

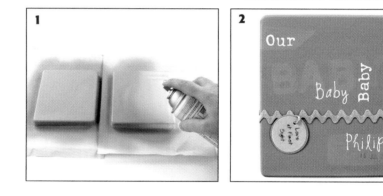

⑤ Score lines every 4½" down the strip of cardstock and fold on these lines in an accordion folded pattern, back-and-forth.

⑥ Use a corner rounder punch to round off the corners at each folded edge.

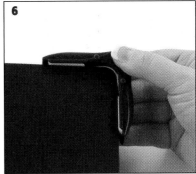

⑦ Use photo tape to attach the back page to the inside of the bottom of the painted case.

⑧ Decorate the cover with a photo that sets the theme of the album. Here the book is about family members meeting a new baby, so the baby photo is the focal point of the cover.

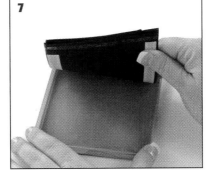

⑨ The inside pages are simply embellished with ribbon, brads, and tags that have the name of each family member. The photo on each page shows that person holding the new baby.

Make a CD Case Album

Scrapbooks do not have to be square or rectangular. This circular album has just enough pages to record the memories of a game night at home and fits inside a clear compact disc container.

MAKING THE ALBUM

1. Start this book by using a compact disc as your template to trace a circle on cardstock for the cover of the album. Cut out this circle of cardstock.

2. Trace and cut more CD-size circles from patterned paper for the inside pages of the book.

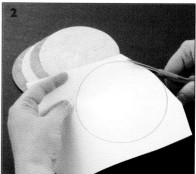

3. Ink the edges of all the cut circles.

4. Stack all the circles together and use a hole punch to create a small hole through all the layers for a brad.

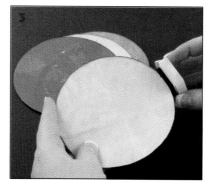
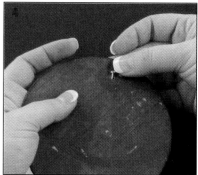

5. Add sticker letters to the cover. Trim the stickers to fit, if needed.

6. Print journaling titles/words on coordinating cardstock or printed paper.

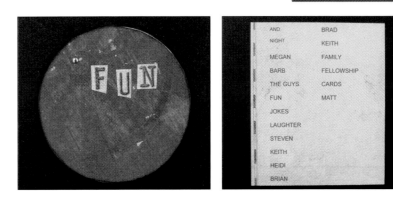

7. Cut out the words and ink the edges of each one. The words can be added as needed on each page with your photos.

8. Slip the album inside the CD case. Embellish the case with spray paint, stickers, or rub-ons if desired. Here the case is left clear so that the mini-book inside can be seen.

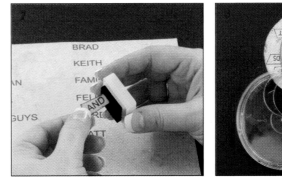

TIP

Look around the house for boxes or cases that can be made into mini-scrapbooks. Jewelry gift boxes, DVD cases, or mint tins are all perfect for mini-scrapbooks. Once completed, these tiny books make great, personalized gifts for any occasion.

14

Photo Inspiration

The focal point of a scrapbook page is a great photo. Manipulating photos by printing them on interesting materials or changing the colors can turn them into pieces of art. Advanced photo techniques make scrapbook pages both unique and interesting. Next time you flip through your pictures, begin thinking about creative ways to display them in your scrapbooks.

The foundation of most of your scrapbook pages is solid cardstock or patterned paper. Get creative with background choices by using your photos as a subtle background statement.

Select a photo that doesn't have a lot of detail. Photos of landscape, architecture, or scenery make great choices. Photos of people might be too busy to be a large background picture.

Enlarge the photo on your computer and print it out on white card-stock using the draft or economy mode on your printer settings.

Tear and chalk the edges of the photo to make it blend into the background of your layout.

Matted photos, journaling boxes, and embellishments can be added to complete the layout. Here the background echoes the photos on the page. Tiny versions of the same photos are framed in slide mounts as embellishments.

Printing or color copying your photos on transparencies gives your pages a whole new texture. In the layout shown here, black-and-white heritage photos have been scanned and printed on a transparency sheet.

The fountain in front of St. Peter's Cathedral, Rome, Italy

rome

Visiting Rome must have been an amazing experience for my great-grandparents. They lived in a small, rural town in Wisconsin. I didn't even know that they made such a trip until I came across these old, family photos. They are like a window to a different time. My Great-grandmother is walking all over Rome, sight-seeing, dressed up in a dress and a pair of heels. Great-grandpa is in his Sunday best suit.

Use special paper-backed fabric to print photos for a look that has texture and a unique finish. The scrapbook page shown here includes a photo of these adorable ballerinas printed on cotton fabric that is lined with paper especially for use in an ink-jet printer.

Mosaic Scrapbook Pages

The traditional art form of mosaics has been around for more than 4,000 years. Although this technique can be time-consuming, photo mosaics create stunning layouts that will be treasured in your albums.

Create Photo Mosaics

1. Select photos that form a cohesive mosaic layout. Avoid pictures that focus on people, choosing instead photos of architecture, landscapes, or scenery.

2. Using a trimmer, a square punch, or a specialty mosaic square template and swivel knife, cut the photos into 1" squares.

③ Adhere the squares to your scrapbook page, leaving an even space between each square. As you attach the photos, mix up the squares from one photo with squares from the next so that the images flow seamlessly.

④ Leave spaces for whole photos, journaling, and embellishments to finish off the scrapbook page.

CONTINUED ON NEXT PAGE

Photo mosaics fit with any theme scrapbook layout. The page shown here uses Christmas photos of a decorated tree and gifts to fill in the space around the larger photos and matted three-dimensional stickers.

The famous pop-art artist Andy Warhol specialized in experimenting with color. Changing the color of a photo can change the entire mood. Use your favorite photo-editing software to adjust the color of your photos before printing them to get results like those shown in this layout, called "The Colors of You."

Blue symbolizes trust, loyalty, wisdom, confidence and intelligence.

Red is associated with energy, strength, determination, spirit & love.

Green is the color of growth, hope, harmony, peace and serenity.

Spot Color Technique

Color can help focus the eye on the important parts of a photograph. In the soccer picture shown here, the goalie's save becomes the focal point when everything else fades into black and white.

Create a Spot of Color

① Open the photo in a photo-editing software program. Microsoft Digital Image Pro 10™ is used for this example. Click on "Edit" and "Selection Tools." Use the Edge Finder selection tool to carefully trace completely around the item in the photo that you wish to keep in color.

② When the item is selected, "cut" it out of the photo by clicking on "Edit" and "Cut."

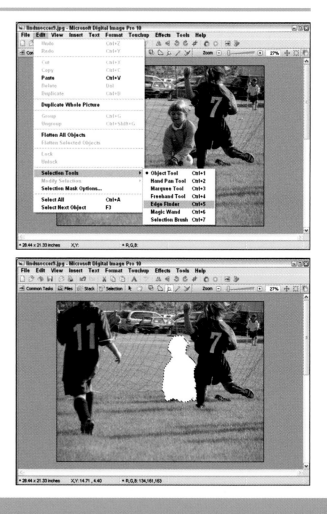

③ Change the rest of the photo to black and white by clicking on "Effects" and then "Black and White."

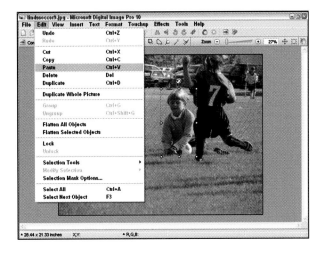

④ Paste the color portion back into the photo by clicking on "Edit" and "Paste." Save and print the photo for use on your scrapbook page.

15

Layout Gallery

As scrapbookers create pages, their personal styles begin to emerge. Each technique learned can be translated by this style to become unique pages that hold cherished memories. The Layout Gallery highlights pages that show off the techniques learned throughout this book. All of them have been interpreted by page designers to become works of art to be displayed in scrapbooks that will be handed down to future generations.

Title: "Utah" by Tracey Eller. **Materials Used:** Paper, license plate, keys – Club Scrap; ribbon – Making Memories; Family Vacation Word – Go West; spiral wire – 7 Gypsies; letters – QuiKutz; inks and glass – Ranger; compass stamps – PSX; tiny compasses - unknown. **Technique to Note:** "Enlarge Your Photos" in Chapter 2.

Title: "Simon" by Mindy Tobias. **Materials Used:** Printed paper – Masterpiece Studios; stickers – Sticker Studio; rubber-stamped letters – Image Tree EK Success. **Technique to Note:** "Take Better Photos" in Chapter 2.

I took you to see Santa for the first time on December 4, 2004. I was afraid you'd be frightened, so I tried to prepare you for what to expect. When I mentioned you'd sit on his lap, you responded by saying you'd give him a hug! When I told you to make sure and tell him what you wanted for Christmas, you said you wanted "Strawberry Shortcake." That morning I had a horrible migraine, but you were so excited that I couldn't bear to tell you to wait another day. We arrived at the post office where Santa was waiting. You gave him a hug and sat on his lap and talked in private whispers so that I couldn't hear. And when we came home, I asked you what you asked Santa for and you looked at me and with a huge smile on your face and said "I want to be a Momma, just like you." And that was when Christmas had come early for me. Thank you Santa!

*Title: "Wish" by Jennifer Okonek. **Materials Used:** Cardstock – Bazzill; printed paper – Melissa Frances; metal frame and letters – Making Memories. **Technique to Note:** "Enlarge Your Photos" in Chapter 2.*

Hi Mindy,

Here's some more little snippets of information on Sarah - Old Bobby. It's based upon what my mother had told me.

At one time, my mother and your maternal grandfather (Martin Wagner), were part of a family of eight children.

As Bobby Matel helped out in the business, Sarah would do some of the cooking for the family.

For Shabbas, she would make little Challahs for each of the children.

There is an old Yom Kippur tradition called "Shlugh Kapporas", which involves the swinging of a live chicken over one's head.

Sarah used to do that, and the children were afraid when she did it.

She did not speak or understand much or any English, but for the most part, she and I were able to understand each other.

She was 90 years old when I was born, yet she had the strength to push me in my carriage.

When I knew her, she did not have any teeth, but her gums were strong enough to crack nuts (that part about the nuts, is from what my mother told me).

She liked to eat chocolate flavored Ex-Lax (a laxative).

Best Regards,

Barry

Also Sarah's maiden last name was Wagner. Before all of our ancestors came to the U.S., the last name was Wagreich. It was changed when one of Sarah's brothers came to the U.S.

The confusion over last names is understandable. In Europe, jewish marriages were often not recognized by civil authorities (another form of prejudice). Therefore, the children of jewish marriages were considered as children born out of wedlock, and thus took the mother's last name. Sarah's last name was Wagreich. Her second husband's last name was actually Gans. Sarah - Old Bobby (I used the term "Bobby" when I referred to or spoke to them. There is a Polish word "Bobshi", which means grandmother)

Our ancestors were from Poland, and that may be why I used the term "Bobby" (a sound similar to "Bobshi").

Sarah died in 1959 and was either 103 or 104 years old when she died. She would not tell her age when she was asked.

Therefore, she was born around 1855.

From what I know, she had three brothers (Benjamin Wagner, Sam Wagner and Mendel Wagner).

She was married three times.

The first marriage was to a man much older than her. She did not like him and would not sleep with him. It was probably an arranged marriage, which was common in those days.

I suppose that first marriage ended in a divorce.

With her second marriage, she had children (Harry Wagner, Sam Wagner (different from the Sam Wagner mentioned above) and Louis Wagner).

She had at least one other child, who probably died at a young age.

From what Aunt Dot (my Mom) told me, she had different occupations: owned a candy store; cooked for other families.

Title: "Old Bubby" by Mindy Tobias. *Materials Used:* Patterned paper – Rusty Pickle, K & Company, Karen Foster Design; cardstock – KMA; nailheads – Magic Scraps; star tile – Sarah Heidt; Grand Parent Tile – Go West; poppy sticker – EK Success. *Technique to Note:* "Get Started Journaling" in Chapter 3.

Title: "Determination" by Michon Kessler. **Materials Used:** Cardstock – Bazzill; printed paper – GinX; ribbon – Offray; rickrack and brads – DoodleBug; flowers, chipboard letter, metal letters – Making Memories. **Technique to Note:** "Create a Focal Point" in Chapter 3.

Title: "Charlie in the Snow" by Jennifer Foster. **Materials Used:** Patterned paper – Daisy D's; cardstock – Die Cuts With a View; label – Dymo; "snow" letters – Scrapworks; snowflake – Making Memories; beads – Stampin' Up; wire – Artistic Wire; corner punch – EK Success; brads – Bazzill; flower punch – EK Success; fonts – Creating Keepsakes; die-cut letter – QuiKutz; glitter. **Technique to Note:** "Using a Color Wheel" in Chapter 4.

Title: "Growing Up Friends" by Jennifer Foster. **Materials Used:** Cardstock – Bazzill; stickers – All My Memories; patterned paper – LaRayne Miller and Keeping Memories Alive; stitching template – Lasting Impressions; library pocket – Jennifer's design. **Technique to Note:** "Library Pocket Journaling" in Chapter 6.

Title: *"Amaizeing Adventure" by Michon Kessler.* **Materials Used:** *Patterned papers – Daisy D's and K & Company; vellum, brads, and textured paper – Provo Craft; antique brads, vellum tag, definition, and metal plaque – Making Memories; sticker – Melissa Francis.* **Technique to Note:** *"Journal on Transparencies" in Chapter 6.*

Title: "Romance" by Michon Kessler. **Materials Used:** Patterned paper and stickers – Pebbles, Inc.; fibers – Fibers By the Yard; heart brads and spirals – 3SD. **Technique to Note:** "Journal on Transparencies" in Chapter 6.

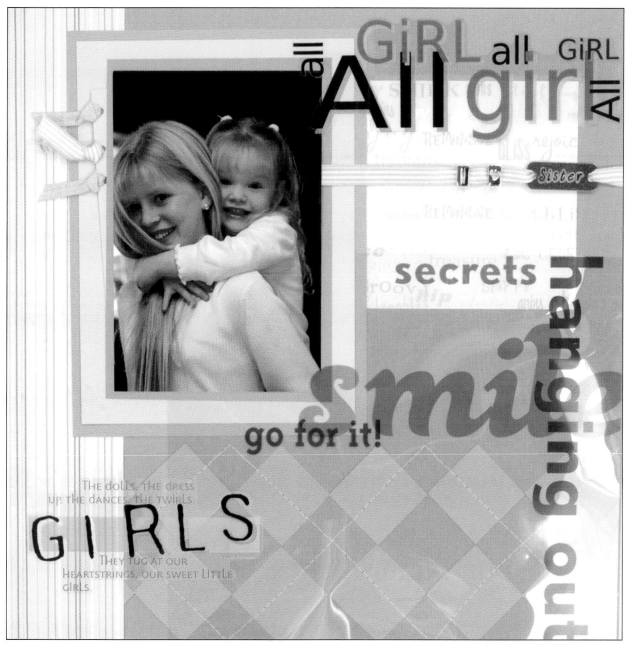

Title: *"Argyle Girls" by Michon Kessler.* **Materials Used:** *Patterned paper – KI and SEI; cardstock – Bazzill; tiny letter stickers and Ratatat font – Provo Craft; charm slide – Making Memories; overlay – Karen Foster Design; clear stickers – Creative Imaginations; charms – MUDD; ribbon – Offray.* **Technique to Note:** *"Photos as Journaling Pockets" in Chapter 6.*

Title: *"Happy Day" by Candy McSween.* **Materials Used:** *Cardstock, printed cardstock, printed words and title –
Wild Asparagus by My Mind's Eye; rub-ons - SEI.* **Technique to Note:** *"File Folders Journaling" in Chapter 6.*

Title: "Dad" by Veronica Johnson. **Materials Used:** Cardstock – Bazzill; printed paper – Chatterbox; chipboard letters and rub-ons – Heidi Swapp; label maker labels – Dymo; foam stamps and paint – Making Memories; rubber stamps – Close to My Heart. **Technique to Note:** "Painted Chipboard Titles" in Chapter 8.

Title: *"Puppies" by Jennifer Foster.* **Materials Used:** *Cardstock – Bazzill; patterned paper – All My Memories; ribbon – Making Memories; buttons – Stampin' Up; computer fonts – Creating Keepsakes and Two Peas in a Bucket; denim fabric and clear transparency – unknown.* **Technique to Note:** *"Die-Cutting Fabric, Cork, and More" in Chapter 8.*

Title: "Back to School" by Jennifer Schmidt. **Materials Used:** Cardstock – The Paper Loft; label maker words – Dymo; die-cut letters and tag – Sizzix; wire – Artistic Wire; brads – ScrapArts.
Technique to Note: "Die-Cut Shaker Titles" in Chapter 8.

NAVY

Robert E. Schultz
Fireman 1st Class
USS Pennsylvania
USS Okaloosa
Service Dates:
January 11, 1943-
February 18, 1946

"Without a decisive naval force we can do nothing definitive, and with it, everything honorable and glorious."
President George Washington

Title: "Navy" by Jennifer Schmidt. **Materials Used:** Printed paper – Fiskars; photo corners – Fiskars and Creative Memories; eyelets – Karen Foster Design; 3-D stickers – K & Company. **Techniques to Note:** "Paper Tearing," "Adding Texture," and "Inking" in Chapter 9.

Title: "Thankful" by Michon Kessler. **Materials Used:** Patterned papers – Gin-X, Karen Foster Design, and Diane's Daughters; stamps – Lil' Davis, Stampin' Up, and Making Memories; Bazzill Boshers; brads – Chatterbox and Making Memories; other – ribbon and gold leafing. **Technique to Note:** "Sewing on Paper" in Chapter 9.

Title: *"Ferry Crossing" by Rebecca Ludens.* **Materials Used:** *Cardstock – Club Scrap; shape punches – EK Success; brads – Making Memories; font – Comic Sans MS and Arial.* **Technique to Note:** *"Geometric Borders" in Chapter 9.*

Title: *"Pickles" by Mindy Tobias.* **Materials Used:** *Printed vellum – K & Company; buttons – Jesse James Buttons; wire – Artistic Wire.* **Technique to Note:** *"Serendipity Squares" in Chapter 9.*

PINK CHEEKS & SNOWMEN

...are two of my favorite things. You guys were so adorable learning the essentials of snowman building from your Dad— a true artist when it comes to snowmen. (wink) From testing the snow for the right stickiness, to the oughtta-be-patented "roll and pat" maneuver, to using the best stuff from our winter garden for our snowman's fabulous features— you two soaked it up like sponges! I'm sure you enjoyed the building part, but its obvious that your favorite part (and Daddy's too) was the winter snuggle you all enjoyed when it was over.

January, 2003 Ken, Amelia, and Eli enjoying a snowy day in our back yard on Garrison.

Title: "Pink Cheeks and Snowmen" by Jenna Tomalka. **Materials Used:** Printed paper – unknown; title font – Lemonade; shrink film. **Technique to Note:** "Paper Tearing" in Chapter 9.

Title: "Melt a Thousand Snows" by Jenna Tomalka. **Materials Used:** Printed paper – Cut It Up; snowflake sequins – Darice; brads and vellum - unknown. **Technique to Note:** "Sewn Vellum Journaling Boxes" in Chapter 9.

Title: *"Bulldog" by Jennifer Schmidt.* **Materials Used:** *Patterned cardstock – The Paper Loft; die-cut letters – Sizzix; circle and square punches – EK Success.* **Technique to Note:** *"Geometric Borders" in Chapter 9.*

Title: *"Back to the Grind Stone" by Tracey Eller.* **Materials Used:** *Paper – Bazzill; rub-ons – My Mind's Eye and Making Memories; ink – Ranger; clips – Creative Impressions; tiles, rings, and anchors – Junkitz.* **Techniques to Note:** *"Paper Tearing" and "Inking" in Chapter 9.*

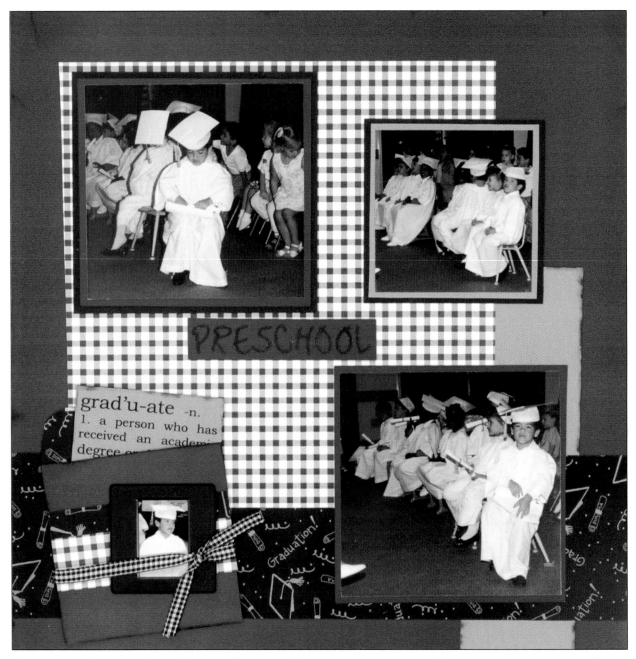

Title: "Preschool Graduate" by Vicki Lockmiller. **Materials Used:** Cardstock – Bazzill; printed paper – unknown; ribbon – Frances Meyer; slide mount – Boxer; library pocket – AccuCut; ink – Ranger; die-cut letters – QuiKutz. **Techniques to Note:** "Library Pocket Journaling" in Chapter 6 and "Slide Mounts" in Chapter 10.

Title: *"Loved" by Jenna Tomalka.* **Materials Used:** *Cardstock and printed cardstock – Club Scrap; buttons and slide mounts – Lumpy Stuff.com.* **Techniques to Note:** *"Journaling on Transparencies" in Chapter 6 and "Slide Mounts" in Chapter 10.*

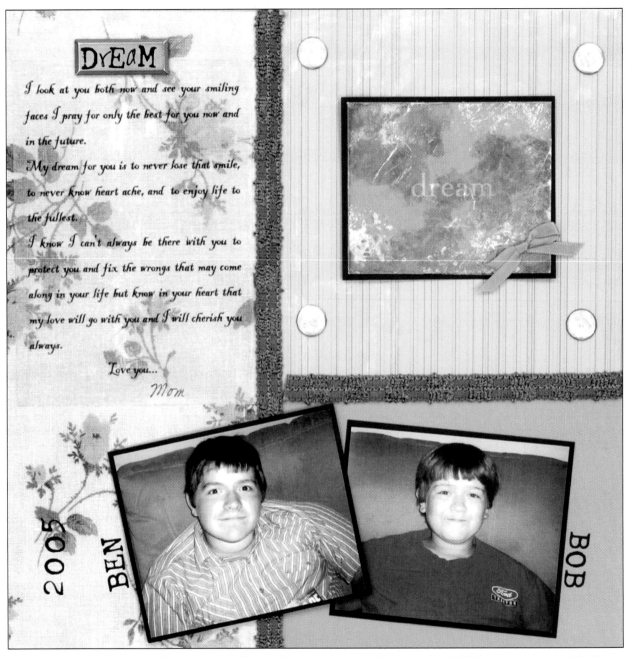

DrEaM

I look at you both now and see your smiling faces I pray for only the best for you now and in the future.

My dream for you is to never lose that smile, to never know heart ache, and to enjoy life to the fullest.

I know I can't always be there with you to protect you and fix the wrongs that may come along in your life but know in your heart that my love will go with you and I will cherish you always.

Love you...

Mom

2005   BEN   dream   BOB

Title: "Dream" by Veronica Johnson. **Materials Used:** Printed paper and cardstock – Wild Asparagus by My Mind's Eye; rub-on letters and accent bar – Making Memories; brads – Karen Foster Design; Mica – USA Quest; trim – Collage Trims Expo International; vellum and pearl paint – unknown. **Technique to Note:** "Fibers" in Chapter 10.

friend (fr'end) *n*. 1. A person that is liked, trusted and cared about 2. A person who is allied for the same cause.

pals

pal (p'al) *n*. 1. A person that is a friend or chum 2. To hang around with someone of like nature

chum

buddy

best friends

pals

best buds

Friends

F*riend*

2004

Title: *"Friend" by Vicki Lockmiller.* **Materials Used:** *Cardstock – Bazzill; Patterned paper – Provo Craft; clips and screw brads – Creative Impressions; rub ons – Making Memories; numbers – QuiKutz.*
Technique to Note: *"Brads" in Chapter 10.*

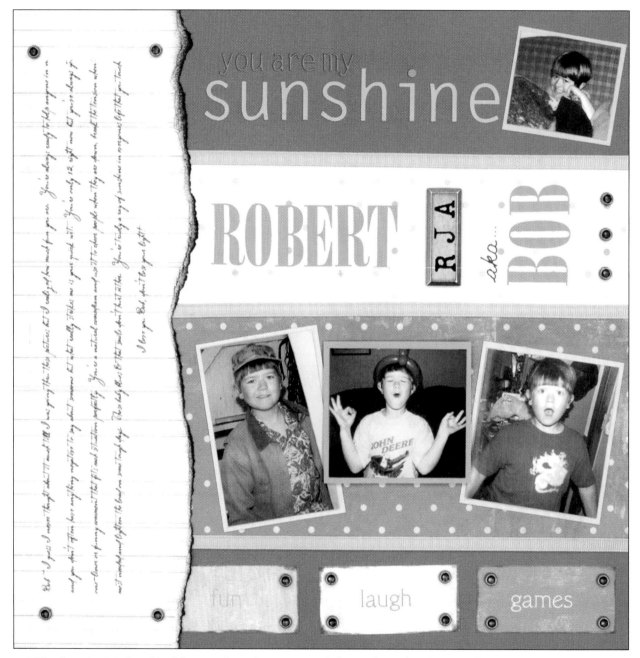

Title: "You Are My Sunshine" by Veronica Johnson. **Materials Used:** Cardstock – Bazzill; printed paper, word tiles, and ribbon – Wild Asparagus by My Mind's Eye; rub-on alpha bar – Making Memories; accent bar – All My Memories; ink – Ranger; metal studs – EK Success. **Technique to Note:** "Eyelets" in Chapter 10.

Title: *"Really Retro" by Veronica Johnson.* **Materials Used:** *Cardstock – Bazzill; patterned paper and buttons – EK Success; flowers and heart brads – Making Memories; hand die-cut – Sizzix; acrylic stamps – MSI; black ink – TAC; fiber and brads – JoAnn's Store.* **Technique to Note:** *"Fibers" in Chapter 10.*

Skinner Lake

relax

R & R

rest

Summer

H-O-T

50% Fun
40% Sweat
10% Water

Wash in Cool

'04

Title: *"R&R" by Veronica Johnson.* **Materials Used:** *Cardstock – Bazzill; printed paper and wave stripe – Sassafrass Lass; stamps – Making Memories; fabric pieces and buttons – Junkitz; travel label – Making Memories.* **Technique to Note:** *"Household Embellishments" in Chapter 10.*

Title: "Perfectly Precious" by Jennifer Okonek. *Materials Used:* Cardstock – Bazzill; words – Scrapworks Hugs; labels – Junkitz; metal stickers – Creek Bank Creations; patterned papers – KI Memories and Provo Craft; vellum title – Quick Quotes; clay phrase – Lil' Davis; other – ribbon, button, jump rings, fibers, eyelets, and brads. *Techniques to Note:* "Eyelets" and "Brads" in Chapter 10.

Title: *"Jewish American Hero"* by Mindy Tobias. **Materials Used:** *Cardstock – Bazzill; printed paper, stickers, and eyelets – Karen Foster Design; buttons – Jesse James Buttons.* **Technique to Note:** *"Eyelets" in Chapter 10.*

Title: *"Bob" by Veronica Johnson.* **Materials Used:** *Cardstock – Bazzill; printed paper – Rusty Pickle; washer – Bazzill Boshers; inks – Ranger; sticker – Karen Foster Design; book darts – Lee Valley; coins – Nostalgiques by EK Success.* **Technique to Note:** *"Photos on Fabric" in Chapter 14.*

Title: *"Castle Ruins" by Neith Juch.* **Materials Used:** *Cardstock – Club Scrap; patterned paper – Slab III; stamps – Making Memories, and Anna Griffin; journaling text – from Geocache website.* **Technique to Note:** *"Photo Backgrounds" in Chapter 14.*

Title: "Spring" by Rebecca Ludens. **Materials Used:** Paper and stickers – The Paper Loft; wire – Artistic Wire. **Technique to Note:** "Wire Words" in Chapter 11.

Appendix

Resource List and Patterns

The popularity of scrapbooking has caused an explosion in the number of companies that manufacture fantastic products. Organizers, tools, papers, stickers, embellishments, adhesives, and albums come in every shape, size, and color. Here you can find the names of the manufacturers whose products were used on the projects throughout this book. Also, you will find the patterns used on several of the scrapbook pages in earlier chapters so that you can re-create these layouts in your own albums.

CHAPTER 1

Open Album: Album: Dalee Book; Preschool Scrapbook Page: Paper – EK Success; Clip art and fonts – Creating Keepsakes; Die cut numbers and letters – Sizzix; Brads and gold thread – unknown.

"Bethany's 13th Birthday" Page: Scrapbook page kit – Hot Off the Press's Almost Done Page Kit Birthday.

"First Car" Page: Patterned paper – Anna Griffin; Font – Times New Roman.

"Shhhhh" Page: Patterned paper – Chatterbox by EK Success; Ribbon – Offray.

Children's Basic Supplies: Trimmer – EK Success; Scissors – Fiskars; Tape runner – 3L; School stickers – Colorbök and Frances Meyer; Solid cardstock – DMD, Inc.

Albums: Navy 5" × 7" – Pioneer; Pink 6" × 6" – Karen Foster Design; Lime 6" × 6" – EK Success.

"Year in Review" Page: Paper and button stickers – EK Success.

"R is for Rachel" Page: Patterned paper – Doodlebug Design, Inc.; Sitckers – Stickopotamus and Jolee's Boutique – EK Success; Font – Times New Roman and TypoUpright BT.

"My Friends" Page: Fonts – Steamer and Arial; paper and flower – unknown.

"Breakfast with Mickey" Page: Solid cardstock – DMD Industries; Phrase stickers – Magical Memories from Phrase Café by EK Success; Mouse sticker – Sandy Lion Sticker Design; Font – Comic Sans MS.

Albums: Black Disney 8" × 8" post-bound album – EK Success; Purple 8" × 8" – Dalee Book; Mulberry 5" × 7" strap-hinge album – Creative Memories; Black 12" × 12" ring-bound album – unknown; Book bound album – Stone Editions, Inc.; Spiral bound albums – DMD Industries; 12" × 12" Book Look album – Karen Foster Design; Blue window 12" × 12" album – Colorbök; Pink 8½" × 11" album – Dalee Book; Green 8½" × 11" album – Pioneer; 11" × 8½" sage green album – EK Success.

"Trains" page: Solid papers – Die Cuts With a View; Metal letters – Colorbök; Eyelets – Karen Foster Design; Font – Comic Sans MS.

Albums: 4" × 4" spiral bound album – DMD Industries; 6" × 6" burgundy album – Karen Foster Design; 6" × 6" black NASCAR album – EK Success; 8" × 8" red M&M album – EK Success; light blue accordion and baby print mini accordion book – handmade (see Chapter 13); Mini magnetic journals – Karen Foster Design.

Solid Cardstock and Printed Papers: Scrapbook Wizard and Close to My Heart.

Specialty Papers: DMD Industries.

Scissors: Black and yellow scissors – EK Success; Decorative scissors and gray scissors – Fiskars.

Trimmers: EK Success and Fiskars.

Shape Cutters: Punches – Marvy (star and circle) and EK Success (tag and heart); Circle Scissors – EK Success.

Tape Runners: Herma by EK Success; 3L; Scotch; Duck by Henkel.

Photo Tabs: Mounting Squares – 3L; Runner – Herma by EK Success.

Adhesive Dots: Glue Dots International; Sticky Dots by Xyron.

Liquid Adhesive: UHU Scrapbookers Pen; Zig by EK Success; and Gem-Tac by Beacon.

Sticker Machines: 150 and 500 Create A Sticker by Xyron.

Journaling: Pens – EK Success; Photo Marking Pencil – Creative Memories; Template, pens, rubber stamp letters, and colored pencils – EK Success; Ink – Vivid!; chalk – Craf-T Products.

CHAPTER 2

Camera: "Joyful Memories" Black and White Page: Designer – Candy McSween; Paper and embellishments – Wild Asparagus by My Mind's Eye; Rub-ons – SEI.

"Beauty" Large Photo Page: Paper and embellishments – EK Success; Quote – Helen Keller; Font – Arial.

"Two Become One" Heritage Page: Printed papers – The Paper Loft; Embellishments – sewing notions; Font – Edwardian Script ITC.

"Look I Did It Myself" Page: Papers – unknown; ribbon – Offray; Die cut letters and swirl – Sizzix; font – Times New Roman.

"First Car" Page: See Chapter 1.

"Bahamas Excursion" Many Photos Page: Patterned papers, travel overlay (transparency), eyelets and charm – Karen Foster Design; Font – Times New Roman.

Photo Organization: Photo Boxes – White plastic snap case and purple and white plastic photo case – Cropper Hopper by Advantus; Blue cardboard box – Michael's; Photo album – Sam's Club; CD – Memorex.

CHAPTER 3

"Back to School" Page: Solid cardstocks – blue and yellow Colorbök, red – DMD, Inc.; Pre-printed embellishments – Color Blocks by Designs by PM; String and buttons – unknown; Font – Times New Roman.

"Soccer" Pages: Solid Cardstock – Die Cuts With a View; Rub-on letters – Making Memories; Fonts – CK Cursive and Arial.

"Love at First Sight" Page: Cardstock – Bazzill; Sticker Definition – EK Success; Tags and Boxes – About.com Scrapbooking Forum Swap.

"Chicago" Page: Printed Cardstock and Tags – The Paper Loft; Brads – ScrapArts; Copper Wire – Artistic Wire; Font – Brush Script.

"Father and Son" Page: Cardstock – DMD Inc.; Patterned Paper – EK Success; Sticker Letters – Sonnets by Creative Imaginations; Flea-market Block and Sonnets Script – Creative Imaginations; My Type Letters – Colorbök; Die-cut letters – Sizzlits Playground Letters; Font – Amazone BT.

"Mini Golf" Page: Cardstock – DMD Inc.; Die-cut letters – Sizzix; Craft Foam; Brads – Making Memories; Font – Tempus Sans ITC.

"Cheekwood Botanical Garden" Page: Cardstocks and acrylic embellishments – ClubScrap; Brads – ScrapArts; Font – Bickley Script; Excerpt of Poem "Spring" – Phoebe Cary.

"Summer Fun" Page: Solid cardstock – The Paper Loft; Printed Paper – unknown; Die-cut spiral – Sizzix; Small punched spirals – EK Success; Font – Chaucer.

CONTINUED ON NEXT PAGE

Stickers: EK Success, Provo Craft, Mrs. Grossman's, Making Memories, and Karen Foster Design.

Die-Cuts: Machines – QuicKutz and AccuCut; Dies – AccuCut and Sizzix; Die-cuts – Ellison and AccuCut.

Pre-Made Embellishments: Magnetic Journal – Karen Foster Design; Quillettes – EK Success; Eyelet Tag Alphabet – Making Memories, Travel Embellishments – Colorbök; Beach Title – EK Success.

Dimensional Items: Fibers – Adornaments by EK Success; Gems – JewelCraft, Ribbon – Offray; Floral Pebbles – unknown; Buttons – EK Success; Bottle Caps – Design Originals; Stone Stickers – Inspirables by EK Success.

Metal Fasteners: Brads, eyelets, nail heads, scrapbook tacks – ScrapArts, JewelCraft, Making Memories, and Chatterbox.

CHAPTER 4

"Baby Face" Page: Solid cardstocks – DMD, Inc.; Square and circle punches – EK Success; Font – TypoUpright BT; Brads – ScrapArts.

"Lake Michigan" Page: Solid cardstocks – DMD, Inc.; Square punch – EK Success; Font – Mistral; Brads – ScrapArts.

"Birthday Wishes" Page: Solid cardstocks – Die Cuts With a View; Font – Tempus Sans ITC.

"Gorgeous" Page: Textured blue and solid peach cardstock – Club Scrap; 3-D Stickers – Colorbök; Fonts – Creating Keepsakes Cursive and Arial.

"Let's Read" Page: Solid cardstocks – DMD, Inc.; Font – Tempus Sans ITC.

"Pool Fun" Page: Solid cardstocks – DMD, Inc.; Circle punch – EK Success; Font – SBC Love Mom.

"At the Beach – Brights" Page: Patterned papers – Scrapbook Wizard; Solid cardstocks – Colorbök; Ribbon – Offray; Nautical Charms – ScrapArts; Font – Arial; Circle punch – EK Success; Tag – own design.

"At the Beach – Muted" Page: Solid cardstocks – Die Cuts With a View; Circle punch – EK Success; Nautical Charms – ScrapArts; Font – Arial.

"Round & Round" Page: Solid cardstocks – DMD Inc.; Brads – ScrapArts; Sticker letters – Colorbök; Circle punch – EK Success; Font – Arial.

"Blue Eyes" Page: Solid cardstocks – Colorbök; Chalk – Craft-T Products; Ink – unknown; Stamps – Stampabilities; Brads – ScrapArts; Font – TypoUpright BT.

CHAPTER 5

"Bubbles" Page: Solid textured cardstock – Die Cuts With a View; Patterned papers – Scrapbook Wizard; Circle sticker letters – Tag Types EK Success; Brads – ScrapArts; Silver metallic paper – DMD, Inc.; Font – Batang.

Quick 6 Photo Mats: Solid navy cardstock – The Paper Loft.

"Soccer" Page: Patterned Paper – The Paper Loft; Soccer shaker kit – JewelCraft; Star Eyelets – ScrapArts.

"Cowboy" Page: Solid and patterned papers – unknown; Cowboy hat charm – ScrapArts; Cowboy title 3-D stickers – Title Waves by EK Success; Font – Trebuchet MS.

Embellished Mat: Solid cardstocks – Colorbök; Flower punch – EK Success; Colored mini-brads – Making Memories.

More Embellished Mats: Solid cardstocks – unknown; Elephant sticker – Mrs. Grossman's; Elephant rubber stamp – Rubber Stampede, Inc.; Elephant rubber stamp – Rubber Stampede, Inc.; Elephant layout: Die-cut letters – Sizzix Fun Serif; Chalk – Craft-T Products; Font – Arial.

CHAPTER 6

Printing on Vellum: Vellum – WorldWin; Cardstock – Bazzill; Brads – ScrapArts; Font – Bradley Hand ITC.

Printing on Transparencies: Transparencies – Laser printer transparencies by Apollo; Cardstock – Bazzill; Brads – ScrapArts; Fonts – Script MT Bold and Comic Sans MS.

"Aunt Chris" Page: Pink printed cardstock – The Paper Loft; Patterned paper – NRN Designs; Flowers – EK Success; Die-cut letters – Sizzix; Fonts – Times New Roman and Knustler Script.

"American Patriotism" Page: Red solid cardstock – The Paper Loft; Blue with stars patterned paper – Hot Off the Press; Red patterned paper – Keeping Memories Alive; Ribbon – Offray; Font – Times New Roman and Freefrm721.

"First Train Ride" Page: Black and red cardstocks – The Paper Loft; Label maker – Dymo.

"Brownie Troop 98" Page: Paper – The Paper Loft; Font – Times New Roman; Stamped letters Susy Ratto EK Success.

"Extreme Files" Page: Patterned cardstock – The Paper Loft; Sticker letters – Creative Imaginations; Font – Times New Roman; Brads – ScrapArts; Paper clips – source unknown.

"Butterfly Kisses" Page: Patterned and solid cardstock – Club Scrap; Font – Lucinda Handwriting; Printed transparency shapes – Club Scrap.

CHAPTER 7

"Frog Hunting" Page: Patterned cardstocks – The Paper Loft; Letter stickers – Colorbök; Bottle caps – Design Originals; Font – Bradley Hand ITC.

"Pretty Pampered Puppy" Page: Designer – Vicki Lockmiller; Printed patterned papers – Provo Craft, Carolee Creations, ColorMate; Bones: Rebecca Sower EK Success It's a Dog's World, Font – unknown.

"Our Little Monkey" Page: Patterned paper – The Paper Loft; Brads – Making Memories; Font – Times New Roman; Ribbon – Offray.

"Bath Time Fun" Page: Designer – Shiela Scott; Cardstock – Bazzill; Ribbon – Offray; Rub-on letters – Making Memories Heida – Small; Font – Creating Keepsakes Journaling; Snaps – Marcella By Kay.

"Guests, Cake, Pinata" Page: Designer – Vicki Lockmiller; Patterned papers – Creative Imaginations, 2 Girls Colorbök; Cardstock – Bazzill; White paint – Palmer; Rub-on letters – Making Memories Hudson.

"Let It Snow" Page: Patterned cardstock – The Paper Loft; Snowflake brads and snowman charm – Oriental Trading Co.; Font – Trebuchet MS.

"Archery" Page: Designer – Veronica Johnson; Cardstock and buttons – Bazzill; Patterned Paper – Rusty Pickle; Green and black paint and round metal-rim tag – Making Memories; Metal leaf stencil – American Traditions; Walnut Distress Ink and Embossing Powder – Ranger; Ribbon – JoAnne's; Twine – unknown.

"Pretty in Pink" Page: Patterned papers – The Paper Loft; Ribbon – unknown; Flowers with buttons – EK Success.

"Just Keep Swimming" Page: Yellow and striped papers, and Mickey and Goofy Snorkeling Stickers – EK Success; Die-cut letters – Sizzix; Letter stickers – Colorbök.

CONTINUED ON NEXT PAGE

CHAPTER 8

Lettering Templates: Templates – EK Success; Rubber stamps – EK Success; Water and sand printed paper – The Paper Loft; Chalks – Deluxe Cuts; Colored Pencils – EK Success; Sea-shell stickers – JewelCraft; Baby photo stickers – Pebbles, Inc.; Ink – Close to My Heart; Leaf punch – EK Success.

Letter Stickers: Stickers – EK Success, Making Memories, and Colorbök; Adhesive runner – 3L Mounting Squares.

Die Cut Lettering and Shakers: Letter and tag dies – Sizzix.

"Dance" Page: Cardstock – DMD, Inc.; Foam – Fibre-craft Materials Corp.; Beads – JewelCraft; Dance shoes – original design; Font – Arial.

"Christmas Toys" Page: Cardstock – DMD, Inc.; Foam – Fibre-craft Materials Corp.; Beads – Westrim Crafts; Patterned paper – Making Memories; Font – Amazone BT.

"Bubble Bath" Page: Patterned paper – NRN Designs; Rub-ons – Making Memories; Paint – Duncan and Plaid Enterprises; Clear Coat Spray – Plaid Enterprises; Font – Curlz MT; Circle punch – EK Success.

"Mother's Day" Page: Flower and letter dies – Sizzix; Patterned paper – The Paper Loft; Craft paint – Plaid Enterprises; Stamps – Stampabilities; Font – CK Bella.

Rubber Stamped Titles: Stamps – Debra Beagle's Performance Art Stamps, Image Tree by EK Success, Alphabet Pixie by PSX, Chunky Stamps by Duncan Enterprises; Ink pad – Superior; Foam letter Stamps – Making Memories.

"Summer Fun" Page: Cardstock – The Paper Loft and Colorbök; Foam stamps – Making Memories; Buttons – unknown.

Metal Letters: Misc. metal letters – Making Memories and Colorbök.

Letters on Brads: Brads – Office Max; "BradWear" Rub-ons – Creative Imaginations; Office rub-on letters – Presto; Water print paper – The Paper Loft.

Clay Letters: Polymer clay – Sculpey; Letter cutters – Wilton; Cruise ship – EK Success.

Die Cutting Fabric and More: Dies – Sizzix Fun Serif and Ransom; Cork – The Board Dudes, Inc.; Foam – Fiber-craft.

Stencil Paste Letters: Stencil and stencil paste – Stencil Ease.

"Doors of Dublin" Page: Printed and solid cardstock – Club Scrap; Stencil and paste – Stencil Ease; Fonts – Arial and Castellar.

CHAPTER 9

"Sun, Sand, and Surf" Page: Paper and sticker letters – The Paper Loft.

"Sleeping Steven" Page: Paper – DMD, Inc.; Brads – Scrap Essentials; Punches – square and circle – EK Success; Font – Chaucer.

"Dream" Page: Papers and vellums – Club Scrap; Eyelet shapes and words – Making Memories; Ink pad – Dauber Duo; Stamp – Club Scrap.

Textures: Sanding Block – PM Designs; Papers – The Paper Loft.

"Boys Toys" Page: Paper – The Paper Loft; Eyelets – Karen Foster Design; Rub-Ons – Making Memories; Font – Times New Roman.

Inking: Black ink pad – Versa Color; Sienna ink pad – Ancient Page by Clearsnap; Three-color ink pad – Stampabilities.

Chalking: Round set – EK Success; 9 square – Close to My Heart; Large set – Deluxe Cuts.

"Going Wild" Page: Pattern – original design; Paper – DMD, Inc.; Brads – ScrapArts; Font – Arial.

"Milham Park" Page: Papers – Die Cuts With a View; Flowers – sewing notions Jo-Ann Fabrics; Yarn and thread – unknown; Stamp letters – PSX.

"Preschool" Page: Papers – EK Success; Clip art title and clip art apples – Creating Keepsakes Font Software; Plastic filler flowers – unknown. On sample steps – apple clip art is from MS Word.

Vellum Flowers: Punch – EK Success Whale of a Punch; Pop-up GlueDots – Glue Dots International; Beads – JewelCraft.

Vellum Pocket: Colored vellum – Club Scrap.

CHAPTER 10

Eyelets: Eyelets – Making Memories; Tags – original design.

Folded Photo Mat Page: Printed papers, transparency, charm, floss, eyelet – Karen Foster Design.

Brads: Heart brads – Making Memories.

"Mount Rushmore" Page: Solid cardstock – DMD, Inc.; Brads – ScrapArts; Die cut letters – QuicKutz.

"Beach" Page: Solid cardstock – The Paper Loft; Paint strips – PM Designs; Brads and charms – ScrapArts; Slide mounts – photography supply; Font – Brush Script.

Embellished Mounts: Glitter – Art Institute Glitter; Buttons – MainStays Crafts; Micro-beads – Magic Scraps; Silver spray paint – Krylon; Rub-on travel words – Making Memories; Patterned paper – unknown; "Dream" definition sticker – Making Memories; Slide mounts – purchased in bulk from photographic supply company.

"Baby Doll" Page: Die cut letters – Sizzix; Ribbon – Offary; Flowers – unknown; Brads – ScrapArts; Square punchs – EK Success; Font – Times New Roman; Ink – Stampabilities.

Fibers: Ribbon – Making Memories and Offray; Yarn – Hot Off The Press; Floss – DMC and Karen Foster Design; Raffis – Pulsar Paper Products and unknown.

"Pumpkin" Page: Letter stencil – Coluzzle; Papers – DMD, Inc.; Patterned Paper – Karen Foster Design; Font – CK Cursive; Pumpkin – original design.

"Kaitlyn Grace" Page: Paper – Creative Imaginations; Floss – DMC; Font – SBC Love Mom.

"Wild Things" Page: Paper – The Paper Loft; Cork and mini-brads – ScrapArts.

"Wishes" Page: Paper and sticker letters – The Paper Loft; Sewing notions and office products – unknown; Ink – Marvy.

Printing on Textures: Cork – ScrapArts; Fabric – DMC; Fonts – Script MT Bold and Elephant.

CHAPTER 11

Wire and Tools: All wire and tools – Artistic Wire.

"Discover Nature" Page: Paper – The Paper Loft; Leaves and printed vellum – Cropper Hopper; Fonts – Monotype Corsiva.

"Lindsey" Page: Paper – The Paper Loft; Quote – A.A. Milne; Beads – Westrim; Glitter – Art Institute; Font – Monotype Corsiva.

"The Many Faces of Rachel" Page: Printed paper – unknown; Beads and gems – JewelCraft; Font – Tempus Sans ITC.

CONTINUED ON NEXT PAGE

CHAPTER 12

Organizers: Rolling tote – XXL™ from Crop in Style; Backpack from Cropper Hopper; The Seat Case from Karen Foster Design; Paper Sticker Binder™ (PSB) from Crop in Style; Navigator™ tote from Crop in Style.

Paper Organizers: Stacking Trays and Peg-able Trays from Display Dynamics; Rolling Tray Base from Display Dynamics; 12"x12" hanging file folders from Cropper Hopper; Rolling file cart by Fellowes; Cubes by Whitmor; Vertical storage boxes from Cropper Hopper; Clear plastic envelopes by Greenbrier International.

Peg board, screws, wood, hinges, and hooks: The Home Depot.

Embellishment Organization: Embellishment Essentials™ Organizer by Cropper Hopper; Spice Rack from Olde Thompson; Round cases and holder from Tidy Crafts.

CHAPTER 13

Mini-book: Paper – Colorbök; Sticker letters – EK Success; Ribbon – Offray.

Tag "Sisters" Book: Printed cardstock, flower brad, and clear definition stickers – Making Memories; Ribbon – Club Scrap.

"Baby" Mini-book on a Page: Pattern Paper – Remember When; Stamps – Stampabilities and EK Success; Font – Times New Roman; Rick Rack – Trimtex; Ribbon – Offray.

Tag "Back to School" Book: Solid double-sided colored cardstock – WorldWin Paper; Ribbon – Offray; Charm – ScrapArts; Sticker letters – Pebbles, Inc.; Ink – Tsukineko.

Envelope "Sun Seeker" Book: Envelopes and rub-on Phrases – Making Memories; Printed papers, paper floss and charm – Karen Foster Design.

Envelope "Russia" Book: Envelopes, rub-on letters and words – Making Memories; Printed travel papers – Design Originals; Closure – Colorbök; Inks – Tsukineko.

Accordion "Butterfly" Book: Printed paper – K & Company; Solid paper – Colorbök; Ribbon – Sheer Creations for Michael's Stores.

Accordion "Extreme Sports" Book: Pattern paper – EK Success; Ribbon – Offray; Sticker words – Creative Imaginations; Metallic fleck paper – Paper Adventures; Sticker letters – EK Success; Photos by Heidi Lachel.

Mini Accordion Christmas Book: Pattern paper – The Paper Patch; Ribbon – Offray; Cross-stitch embellishments – handmade; Charms – ScrapArts; Brads and eyelets – ScrapArts; Paperclips – unknown; Bookplate – Jo-Ann Stores, Inc.

Paper Bag "Anniversary" Book: Pattern Paper – Creative Imaginations, Design Originals, Fiskars, EK Success, and K & Company; Metallic fleck paper – Paper Adventures; Font – Storybook; Die-cut letters – Sizzix; Rub-ons – Making Memories; Leather frame – Making Memories; Charms – ScrapArts; Sticker letters – EK Success; Ink – Stampabilities; Eyelets – Karen Foster Design; Ribbon – Offray.

Paper Bag "Friends" Book: Patterned Paper – American Crafts; Paint chips – Behr Paints; Silk flowers – Jo-Ann Stores, Inc.; Eyelets and brads – ScrapArts; Rub-ons – Making Memories; Ribbon – Minnesota Mining & Manufacturing Co.

Sizzix Container Baby Book: Box – Sizzix Die container; Spray paint – Plasti-kote Co., Inc.; Rub-ons – Making Memories; Rickrack – Trimtex; Brads – ScrapArts; Wire – Artistic Wire; Acrylic paint – Plaid Enterprises, Inc.; Font – SBC Love Mom; Paper clips – unknown; Circle punches – EK Success; Metallic paper – Paper Adventures.

Round CD Container "Fun and Games" Book: Patter paper and cardstock – The Paper Loft; Sticker letters – The Paper Loft; Brads – ScrapArts; Container – CD case unknown; Font – Arial.

CHAPTER 14

Chalks: Deluxe Cuts.

"The Badlands" Page: Die cut letters – Dayco and QuicKutz; Slide mounts – Magic Scraps; Solid cardstock – WorldWin Paper.

"Trip of a Lifetime" Page: Paper and ribbon – Design Originals; Square mini-brads – ScrapArts; Brad letters – Colorbök; Fonts – Gigi and Arial; Fabric for ink jet printer – The Vintage Workshop.

"A Pair of Ballerinas" Page: Paper – The Paper Loft; Decorative brads – Making Memories; Font – Gigi; Slide letters and strip – Karen Foster Design; Inkjet printable cotton canvas – The Vintage Workshop.

"Christmas" Page: Paper – Wish in the Wind; Die cut letters – QuicKutz; Stickers – Jolee's by EK Success.

"The Colors of You" Page: Designer – Veronica Johnson; Paper – Bazzill; Ribbon – Offray; Rub-on letters, paint, and foam letter stamps – Making Memories; Acrylic colored rectangles – Junkitz; Rub-on letters – Lil' Davis; Word Rub-ons – Deja Views.

CHAPTER 15

Supplies and designers are listed with each scrapbook page.

TAGS

VELLUM POCKET

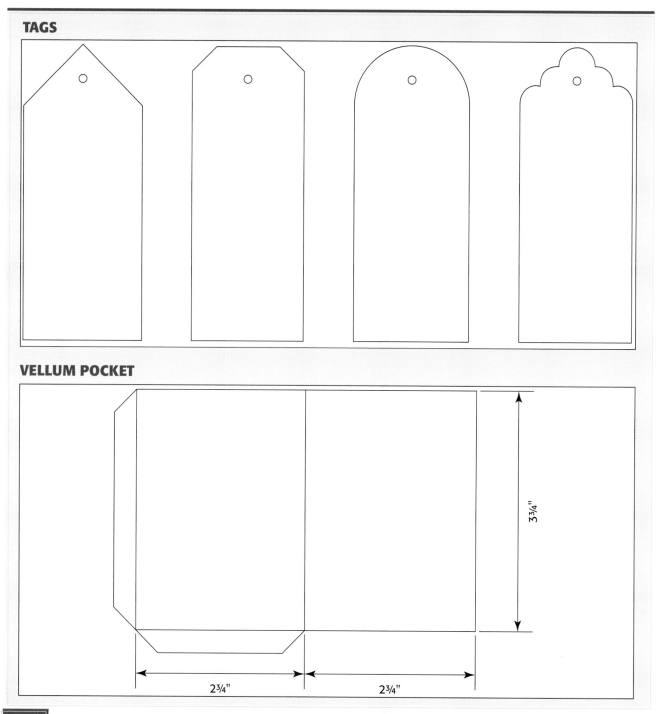

2³⁄₄"

2³⁄₄"

3³⁄₄"

FILE FOLDER

LIBRARY POCKET

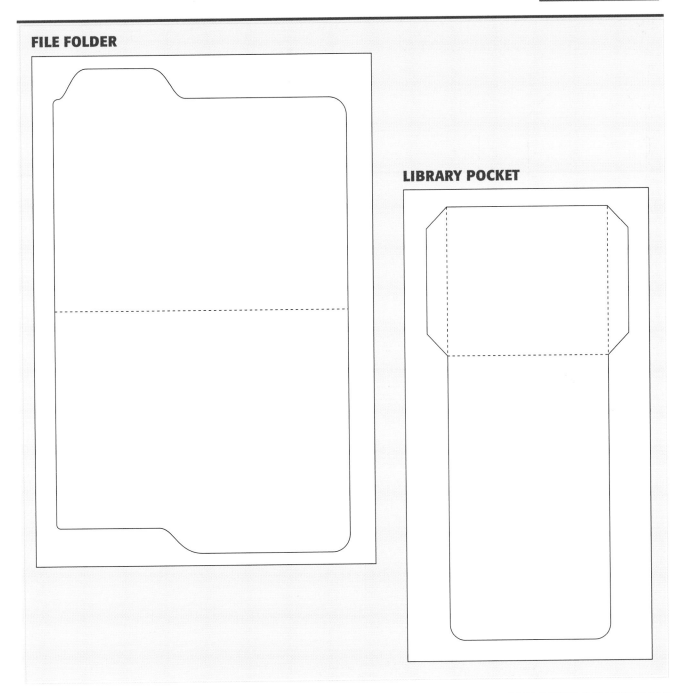

CONTINUED ON NEXT PAGE

MATCHBOOK

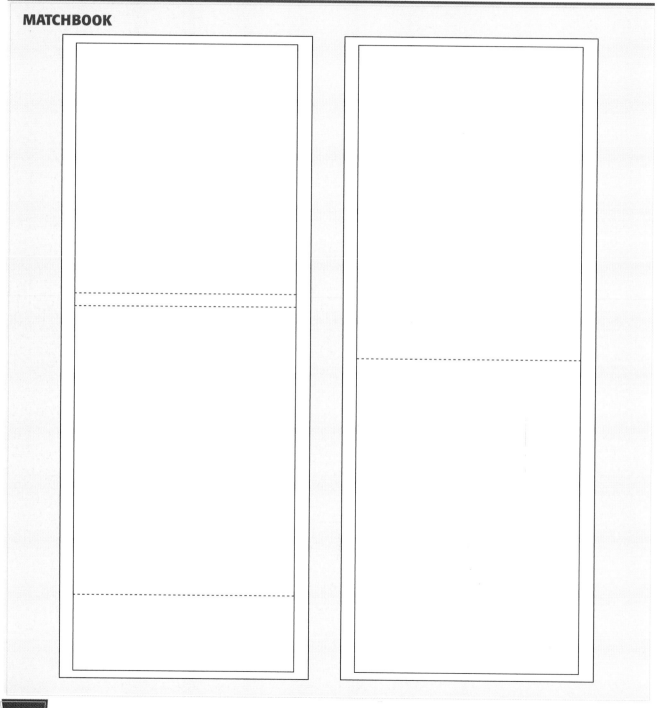

PAPER PIECING

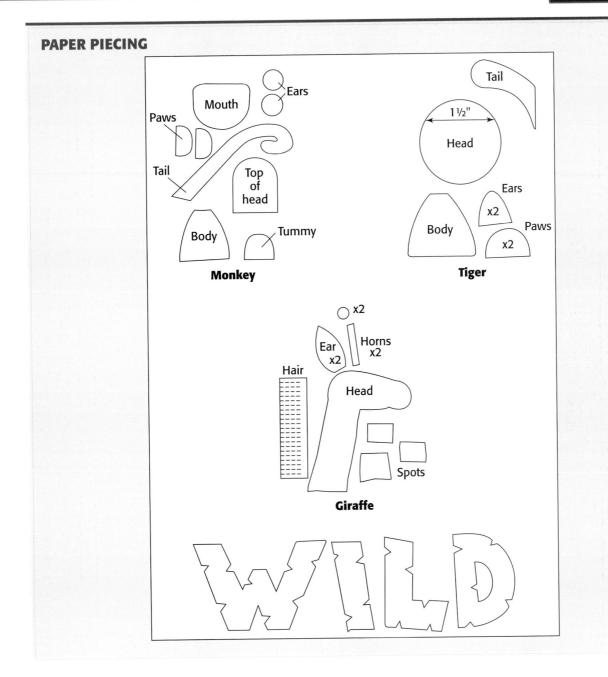

Ears

Mouth

Paws

Tail

Top of head

Body

Tummy

Monkey

Tail

1½"

Head

Ears x2

Body

Paws x2

Tiger

x2

Ear x2

Horns x2

Hair

Head

Spots

Giraffe

WILD

Index

Teach Yourself VISUALLY™ books...

Whether you want to knit, sew, or crochet...strum a guitar or play the piano...train a dog or create a scrapbook...make the most of Windows XP or touch up your Photoshop CS2 skills, Teach Yourself VISUALLY books get you into action instead of bogging you down in lengthy instructions. All Teach Yourself VISUALLY books are written by experts on the subject and feature:

- Hundreds of color photos or screenshots that demonstrate each step or skill

- Step-by-step instructions accompanying each photo
- FAQs that answer common questions and suggest solutions to common problems
- Information about each skill clearly presented on a two- or four-page spread so you can learn by seeing and doing
- A design that makes it easy to review a particular topic

Look for Teach Yourself VISUALLY books to help you learn a variety of skills—all with the proven visual learning approaches you enjoyed in this book.

0-7645-9641-1

Teach Yourself VISUALLY™ Crocheting

Picture yourself crocheting accessories, garments, and great home décor items. It's a relaxing hobby, and this is the relaxing way to learn! This Visual guide *shows* you the basics, beginning with the tools and materials needed and the basic stitches, then progresses through following patterns, creating motifs and fun shapes, and finishing details. A variety of patterns gets you started, and more advanced patterns get you hooked!

0-7645-9640-3

Teach Yourself VISUALLY™ Knitting

Get yourself some yarn and needles and get clicking! This Visual guide *shows* you the basics of knitting—photo by photo and stitch by stitch. You begin with the basic knit and purl patterns and advance to bobbles, knots, cables, openwork, and finishing techniques—knitting as you go. With fun, innovative patterns from top designer Sharon Turner, you'll be creating masterpieces in no time!

0-7645-9642-X

Teach Yourself VISUALLY™ Guitar

Pick up this book and a guitar and start strumming! *Teach Yourself VISUALLY Guitar* shows you the basics photo by photo and note by note. You begin with essential chords and techniques and progress through suspensions, bass runs, hammer-ons, and barre chords. As you learn to read chord charts, tablature, and lead sheets, you can play any number of songs, from rock to folk to country. The chord chart and scale appendices are ready references for use long after you master the basics.

designed for visual learners like you!

0-7645-7927-4

Teach Yourself VISUALLY Windows XP, 2nd Edition

Clear step-by-step screenshots *show* you how to tackle more than 150 Windows XP tasks. Learn how to draw, fill, and edit shapes, set up and secure an Internet account, load images from a digital camera, copy tracks from music CDs, defragment your hard drive, and more.

0-7645-8840-0

Teach Yourself VISUALLY Photoshop CS2

Clear step-by-step screenshots *show* you how to tackle more than 150 Photoshop CS2 tasks. Learn how to import images from digital cameras, repair damaged photos, browse and sort images in Bridge, change image size and resolution, paint and draw with color, create duotone images, apply layer and filter effects, and more.

Available wherever books are sold.

Visual
An Imprint of **WILEY**
Now you know.